Raising
Rabbits
Successfully

Raising Rabbits Successfully

Bob Bennett

WILLIAMSON PUBLISHING CO.

CHARLOTTE, VERMONT 05445

Library of Congress Cataloging in Publication Data

Bennett, Bob.
   Raising rabbits successfully.

   1. Rabbits.   I. Title.
SF453.B458   1984   636′.9322   83-27334
ISBN 0-913589-03-9

Cover and interior design: Trezzo-Braren Studio
Photography: By the author except the following
   Safeguard Mfg.: pp. 24, 46, 47, 48, 55, 56, 57, 71, 111
   Ralston Purina Co.: p. 28
   Alice Bennett: pp. 51, 174
   Ted Gordon: pp. 138, 141
   Cover: Three Views of Florida White buck, by author
Printing: Capital City Press

Williamson Publishing
Charlotte, Vermont 05445

Manufactured in the United States of America

10 9 8 7 6 5 4

This book is dedicated to
Dorothy Winifred Bennett
(1913–1983)

Acknowledgements

It is impossible to list the many rabbit breeders across the country who have contributed their ideas and knowledge about rabbits to one who has spent years collecting it from them. Special thanks must be accorded the following persons, however, for their special assistance: Alice, Robert, John and Alyssa Bennett; Anthony Pisanelli, Robert Noble, Jack Williamson, Roger Griffith, Peggy Blanchette, Cathy Baker Snelling, Ken and Loretta Braren, Andrea Chesman, Warren Burrows and Marty Muckenschable.

Contents

Introduction

A lot of people don't know any more about rabbits beyond Peter, Bugs, Easter bunnies, and jokes about their reproductive powers.

In this book I'm going to describe three of the best things rabbits can do for you, have done for me, and have done for others for many years.

1. Put some of the most delicious and, indisputably, the most nutritious and digestible meat on your dinner table.

2. Provide the basis for a part-time or even full-time business that you can start with less than $100.

3. Introduce you to the world of competitive rabbit exhibitions that not only provide fun for the whole family, but inject a sporting note to your rabbit pursuit while spurring an interest in genetics.

Over the past 35 years, off and on, whenever I could, I have raised a number of different breeds. Two of the very best are the ones I describe in this book, the New Zealand White and the Florida White. If you will choose one or the other (or both), and feed and house them following my instructions, you likely will garner some of the same satisfaction and material rewards that rabbits have brought me.

No, I'm not wealthy, and rabbits won't, in all likelihood, make you a millionnaire. But here are just some of the things rabbits have produced at my place:

Tasty dinners, fun, and fascination, and new friends, and extra cash to buy a 10-speed bike, a color television set, a grandfather clock, mahogany Queen Anne furniture, a vacation at Disneyland, four years at the state university, ballet, theatre and baseball tickets, a tractor, dinners out, a rototiller and a bamboo flyrod. I almost forgot the 35 millimeter camera equipment, the snowblower, and the power woodworking tools. Oh, yes, and the barn I keep them in.

Meanwhile, they have never stood in the way of my other hobbies, trips, or family life. So I guess you can see that I think rabbits have been worth the effort. And I'm sure you will find, once you spend a little time with them, even more than three reasons for raising rabbits.

Chapter 1

What You Ought to Know About Rabbit Meat

Vegetables emerge noiselessly from seed. They push up unobtrusively, barely noticed at first, always quiet. They emit no bad odors. Kept weeded, they are neat and attractive. Anyone with even a tiny patch of ground can grow at least a few in almost any climate. Millions of people do.

For most of us, however, vegetables make only part of the meal. The least expensive part. The supplemental, accessory part. Meat plays the main-dish role and it carries the biggest price tag.

Growing your own vegetables is quite feasible, but raising your own cattle, hogs or even chickens is out of the question for many. It takes lots of land, zoned for agriculture, and a big investment of money and time. So, many persons are forced to purchase all of their own meat.

Or are they? Are you?

You could raise rabbits, in a small place, with no odor and no mess and no noise. Here is an animal equally at home on the farm **and** in the city and town.

In the space your kitchen table occupies you can produce up to 100 pounds of dressed, delicious rabbit meat annually at an average cost of as little as 20 to 50 cents a pound or even less. It's a high-quality specialty delicacy—a gourmet product that sells for $3 a pound and more in the nation's supermarkets.

Facts About the Meat

Here are the facts about rabbit meat:

It is wholesome and nutritious. It is all-white meat. It has more protein, less fat, less cholesterol, and fewer calories, pound for pound, than any other meat you can buy. It will do you more good and less harm than any other meat.

And, boy, does it taste good!

You can bake it, broil it, roast it, stew it, or fry it. Good cooks prepare rabbit according to recipes that call for veal and chicken. Delicious dishes can be produced either on short notice or with lengthy, loving preparation.

Some of the best recipes originated in Europe along with much of the rest of the world's best cuisine. The French, the Germans, and the Italians all have contributed excellent recipes for rabbit even as they have set the pace for **haute cuisine** that is followed all over the world.

Others are of Oriental origin. Chinese, Japanese, and Polynesian dishes can be prepared with rabbit meat and vegetables just as they are in the best Oriental restaurants. Not to be left out are the Americans. Plenty of fine recipes, including Southern fried rabbit, Texas barbecued rabbit, rabbit pie, and others reflect the regional tastes and customs of the United States.

Why then, you might well ask, is rabbit meat so well loved in European and other countries but largely unknown in the United States? Why is rabbit one of the best kept dinner table secrets in the country?

Here are some of the reasons. One has to do with refrigeration. Would you consider the simple ice cube, mere frozen water in a tray, the equal of a gleaming diamond? Hardly. But if you lived in much of the world, perhaps around the Mediterranean or Caribbean seas, in southern Europe, Africa, or Latin America, an ice cube could be almost as precious. In the United States we take refrigeration for granted. We can butcher a large animal, eat some of it now, and store some for later. Refrigeration makes it possible. In other places, if you want meat, you eat it all right now. That means a feast of luau proportions or a small animal. Like a rabbit. You store it on the hoof until you are ready to eat it all.

Another has to do with space. Cattle and hogs are raised on huge ranches and farms. They consume hundreds of bushels of grain grown on thousands of acres. Even more compact cattle feedlots and confinement hog operations must be away from population centers because of the smell and the noise. In the United States we have always had the space and most of us have had the money. In Europe there is little space and for years, particularly in time of war, very little money.

In large part it was war that kept rabbit meat on European tables for centuries. Invading armies invariably drove off or slaughtered cattle, sheep, and hogs. They couldn't catch the domesticated but fleet rabbits that inhabited the farmers' barns, living off feed left over by the larger animals.

Popular During War

World War II brought rabbits some prominence in the United States. Because meat was rationed, with each family being allocated stamps that had to be presented when buying fresh meat at the market, Americans were faced with meatless meals. Or nearly meatless. How we learned to loath the canned processed meats such as Spam and Prem, the butt of countless jokes. Thousands of resourceful Americans raised rabbits in backyards to put meat on the table when ration stamps were not sufficient to do the job. In cities and towns, in the best of neighborhoods, rabbits were housed in wood and chicken wire hutches, busily putting meat on their owners' tables. Cattle, sheep, and hogs—even chickens with their cackling and crowing—would never do. Zoning boards wouldn't, literally, hear of it. Think, now, what sound does a rabbit make? Right. I never heard it either.

Today, when so many of us have expressed the desire to produce our own food, largely with vegetable gardens, the rabbit is making a well-deserved comeback. The timing couldn't be better. Many people are looking for a way to put healthful meat on their tables. They are fearful of additives in meat and wish to control meat production themselves.

The rabbit, prepared rabbit feed pellets, and the sanitary cages in which they are raised in the 1980s make it possible for millions of people, living in cities and towns as well as rural areas, to put meat on their tables for pennies a pound, with a small out-of-pocket investment and very little time—and most of that enjoyable.

Chapter 2

The Taste Test

If you think you would like to raise rabbits for your own table, to feed yourself and your family, but need some convincing, nothing beats the taste test. Try it first, to see if you like it.

Go to the supermarket and buy yourself some rabbit. Cook it using one of the following recipes. Let your taste buds be the judge. Then and only then will you be convinced how delicious this nutritious meat can be. Only then will you want to raise your own just as easily as you can raise all the carrots, tomatoes, potatoes, onions, and other vegetables that make a wonderful meal.

The following recipes are not the only ones available. Nor are they necessarily the best. They are my "convincers." These are recipes that are easy to follow, and guide you to make meals that are wonderful to behold, and delicious to eat. I win you over with these—you, the children, whoever does the cooking at your place.

Whole books of rabbit recipes have been published, and I'm going to recommend one in the back of this book. If you try one of the recipes—or more—in this chapter and go on to raise rabbits for your table, you probably will want to buy a good rabbit cookbook. The most observant and creative cooks will notice that these recipes and others resemble those featuring chicken and veal. Instead of trying one of my convincers you might want to try one of your favorite chicken or veal recipes and see how much **better** it can be.

When you get to the supermarket, you may have trouble finding fresh rabbit. Go to the frozen food department and look for it along with the Cornish game hens and other frozen meat specialty or gourmet items. You will probably see it in a yellow box under the brand name "Pel-Freez."

If you can't find rabbit in your supermarket, visit your local feed store and ask the dealer for the name of someone who sells meat rabbits. He probably has some feed customers who sell it right from their homes to a select list of regular customers. He'll be happy to identify one or more of these rabbit raisers for you.

Packaged, frozen rabbit from supermarket.

BAKED RABBIT AND MUSHROOMS

1   fryer rabbit (2½–3 lbs.), cut up
2   tablespoons oil
½   teaspoon salt
½   teaspoon pepper
1   clove of garlic, minced
    Juice of ½ lemon
½   cup sherry wine
1   can cream of mushroom soup
1   cup sliced fresh mushrooms

Mix pieces together with oil, salt, pepper, garlic, and lemon juice; let stand 10–20 minutes. Rub well into rabbit. Arrange pieces in pan. Bake at 450° for 10 minutes. Lower temperature to 350° and continue baking for 15 minutes. Then add ¼ cup of sherry, the can of soup, mushrooms, and bake another 15 minutes. Add rest of wine and cook until rabbit is tender. Length of time depends on size and age of rabbit.

Serves 4

RABBIT CACCIATORE

1   rabbit (2½–3 lbs.), cut up
    Oil
2   onions, sliced
2   garlic cloves, minced
2   cups canned tomatoes (1 #3 can)
1   can tomato sauce (8 oz.)
1   teaspoon salt
¼   teaspoon pepper
½   teaspoon celery seed
1   teaspoon oregano
1   bay leaf
½   cup dry white wine

Brown rabbit in hot oil (use large, deep skillet), remove, and keep hot. Cook onions and garlic in oil until tender. Add other ingredients except wine; cook for 5 minutes. Return rabbit to skillet, cover, and simmer for 45 minutes or until tender. Add wine and cook, uncovered, for 15 minutes. Remove bay leaf. Serve with spaghetti or noodles.

Serves 4

RABBIT CASSEROLE

(This recipe won a statewide 4-H contest in Texas)

- 2 fryer rabbits (about 2 pounds each), cut up
- 4 slices bacon
- 3 medium-size onions, quartered
- 2 green peppers, cut up
- 1 clove garlic, crushed
- ½ cup white wine
- 1 can (1 pound) whole tomatoes
- 1 can condensed cream of mushroom soup
- 1 teaspoon salt
- 1 teaspoon marjoram, crushed
- 1 teaspoon thyme, crushed

Saute bacon until crisp. Drain on paper towels and set aside. Brown rabbit a few pieces at a time in bacon drippings, then arrange in a 2–3 quart baking or casserole dish. Add onion, green pepper, and garlic to same skillet. Add wine. Cook, stirring in and crushing tomatoes, until slightly thickened (about 5 minutes). Stir in cream of mushroom soup, salt, marjoram, and thyme. Heat to boiling, stirring frequently. Spoon over rabbit in baking dish and cover.

Bake at 350° for 1 hour or until rabbit is tender. Just before serving, crumble reserved bacon and sprinkle over the rabbit and vegetables. Serve with hot buttered rice or noodles.

Serves 6

SAUTEED RABBIT LIVERS

(One of my very favorite recipes)

4 rabbit livers
½ teaspoon salt
⅛ teaspoon pepper
2 tablespoons flour
1 finely diced onion
1 tablespoon fat or oil
½ cup bouillon

Cut livers into thirds or quarters. Put salt, pepper, flour into brown paper bag. Shake until mixed. Put in liver pieces and shake until coated. Saute onion in fat or oil. Add livers and brown.

Add bouillon and simmer 3 to 5 minutes. Serve on toast points.

Serves 2 (or eat it all yourself).

STIR-FRIED RABBIT

1 young rabbit (2½–3 lbs.), cut into bite-size pieces
2 tablespoons sugar
2 tablespoons cornstarch
½ teaspoon ginger
3 tablespoons soy sauce
3 tablespoons oil
1 cup thinly sliced carrots
2 cups diagonally sliced broccoli
1 cup chicken bouillon
1 medium onion, thinly sliced
½ cup thinly sliced fresh mushrooms

In medium bowl, combine sugar, cornstarch, ginger, and soy sauce; mix well. Add rabbit pieces; stir to coat. Let stand at least 15 minutes. In large skillet or wok, heat oil over very high heat. Add carrots and broccoli, stir lightly to coat with oil. Add bouillon; cover and cook 2 minutes. Add rabbit and marinade. Stir gently over medium heat until tender. Add onion, mushrooms; stir fry about 1 minute. Serve with rice.

Serves 4

RABBIT BAKED WITH WINE

1   rabbit (2½–3 lbs.), cut into serving pieces
    Juice of one lemon
    Flour
    Salt
    Pepper
¼   cup butter
1   tablespoon chopped parsley
1   tablespoon chopped shallots (or scallions)
1   cup sliced fresh mushrooms
2   cups dry white wine

Sprinkle rabbit pieces with lemon juice; then mix flour, salt, and pepper and coat rabbit pieces. Brown rabbit in ¼ cup butter; add parsley, shallots, and mushrooms and sauté lightly. Remove rabbit pieces and place in baking dish. Add one cup of wine and drippings from pan. Bake uncovered in 325° oven. Use remaining cup of wine for basting. Do not let rabbit dry out. Bake until tender and wine sauce has thickened; approximately 45 minutes.

Serves 4

Chapter 3

The First Key to Success: The Right Rabbit

The combination of proven breeding rabbits, modern, self-cleaning, and sanitary all-wire cages, and the complete feed pellets available from coast to coast make raising rabbits not only possible and plausible but easy and enjoyable. Choosing the **right rabbit**, the **right housing** and the **right feed** are the three keys to success. We will examine all three of these vital facets of rabbit production. First, let's look at the rabbits you should choose. There are two choices, large and small, and two breeds recommended to take you to your objective—meat on your table for pennies a pound.

New Zealand Whites

The larger of the two recommended breeds is the New Zealand White. It is the nation's best-bred, most widely available, and, in fact, best-performing rabbit. More people have raised more New Zealand Whites than any other breed for many years and their efforts have resulted in a rabbit that is your best bet for success. Let's look at this animal in detail.

New Zealand Whites on judging table.

The New Zealand White weighs 10–12 pounds at maturity, which occurs at 6–8 months of age. At 8 weeks, youngsters will weigh 4 pounds or more live weight, and dress out at 2–2½ pounds of delicious, all-white, fine-grained, and small-boned meat.

Whenever you see or hear of a big white rabbit, it's probably the New Zealand White (although there are some rather rare and less suitable big white rabbits, including the Beveren and the Flemish Giant). If there could be only one breed of rabbit, the New Zealand White would be the best bet. It is the hands-down, no-argument, single best rabbit in the world if consistent performance, plenty of meat on little bone, a pelt in demand, and a laboratory market are considered.

If you buy rabbit meat in a supermarket or enjoy it in a restaurant, undoubtedly it is a New Zealand White. It is also the most widely available rabbit. If you follow the recommendations in this book and obtain one New Zealand White buck and two does, you can expect to produce **at least** 128 pounds of dressed, edible meat for your table per year in 2-pound "packages" at a time. In other words, you can expect at least four litters of eight rabbits each per year per doe. Dressed at weaning time you're talking about at least two pounds of meat per rabbit.

With thirty-two rabbits per doe or sixty-four in all, that's 128 pounds. You can, in fact, **double** that amount yearly. But taking into account your probable inexperience, the 128-pounds target is a good one for your first year. And that may be plenty, or even more than enough. Yet there are recipes that let you utilize rabbit meat as sausage for breakfast and sandwich spread or salad for bagged lunches and you will find it creeping into your mealtimes more and more. I should have said hopping into them, of course. Chicken, veal, and even tuna fish may disappear from your table. At least, they will make less frequent appearances because the versatile rabbit will stay one step, er, hop, ahead of them all.

Let's suppose, however, that you don't wish to produce that much rabbit per year. Sure, you could eliminate one doe and produce 64 pounds a year. Or, you could turn to the Florida White.

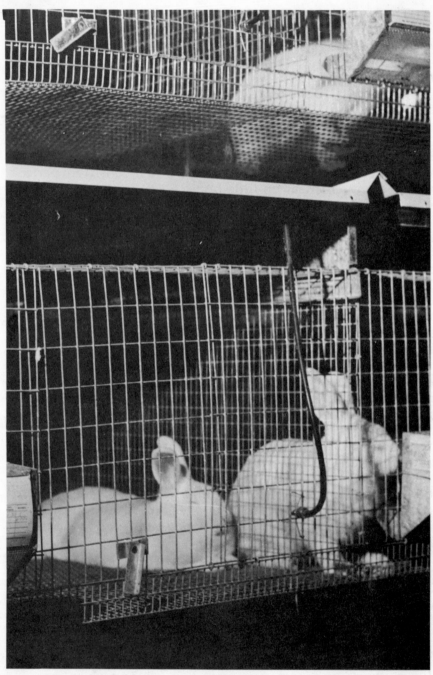

New Zealand Whites in wire hutches.

Florida White.

Florida Whites

The Florida White is a junior size New Zealand. At maturity it weighs about 5 pounds, compared to the New Zealand's 10. It was developed only about 20 years ago by crossing some small rabbits with the New Zealand and then breeding for maximum meat on minimum frame. The result is a solid little performer that will produce not just half, but more likely two-thirds of the meat that the New Zealand will, and that's only part of the story. The best part is that it will do it on half the feed and in little more than half the space.

Florida White.

At 8 weeks, you will get only 1¼–1½ pounds of meat from the Florida White, compared to 2–2½ pounds for the New Zealand White. If you are raising rabbits for only one or two people, this is ideal. On the other hand, if you feed Floridas for another 4 weeks, you will wind up with a full 2 pounds of meat, as much as the New Zealand delivers four weeks earlier. While you wait longer, you don't feed any more, perhaps less, and the required hutch space is also less. You can take your pick—a pound of meat now that is plenty for two people, or a couple of pounds 4 weeks later—fine for a family of four or even five.

During World War II the U.S. Navy included both rabbit and chicken on the menu. A hearty portion of rabbit for a sailor was 6 ounces, compared to 8 ounces of chicken. The reason for the difference lies in the density or texture of the meat, as well as the fineness of bone. Rabbit meat is more filling and there is less bone per serving. So when we talk about a pound or 24 ounces of meat on an 8-week Florida White, we are talking about plenty to eat for a couple of people.

The Florida White is an amazing little rabbit that really has no peer pound for pound. It produces a lot of meat on a small frame in a small space on very little feed. It has a pelt that rivals that of the New Zealand, and it also merits similar demand as a laboratory animal. The fact is that laboratory rabbit buyers don't know the difference between the two in most instances. They want a white rabbit. Period.

Determining factors thus are two—the size of the family that will be eating the meat and the number of times the family wants to eat it.

Crossing Breeds

It may interest you to know that some rabbit raisers use a rather smallish New Zealand buck and a large-type Florida White doe. This cross produces a larger rabbit than the Florida White without the need to provide much extra feed or hutch space. A further refinement is a hybrid situation that utilizes Flemish Giant (very large, 15-pound) bucks, and does that are half New Zealand and half Florida White. The advantages are bigger carcasses in smaller spaces, and less feed for the small does than for bigger ones. Hybrid vigor and unusually good disease resistance are further reasons for following these methods.

The hazard: using a small doe and a large buck can be dangerous to the doe when she gives birth to rather large offspring. Selection of does with well-developed loins and hindquarters lessens the danger that overly large babies will tax her physique to the point of death.

If you are able to obtain rabbits from a breeder who is successful at crossing large and small breeds you may well want to try this approach, which brings us to a critical juncture: how and where to obtain your rabbits and how much to pay.

First, let's look at some approaches not to use. Don't take free rabbits just because you can get them. They could wind up costing you lots more money, feed, time, and grief than those you will carefully choose and willingly purchase.

Your rabbits must come from a breeder who has been producing them successfully and reaching the goal you have in mind. The rabbits you get must be from a healthy, productive herd. This is especially important if you will have only two does and a buck, as suggested here. In a large rabbitry you have more margin for error. A small one must be very efficient. Each rabbit must pull its weight or the whole plan will collapse.

Be very skeptical of free rabbits, cheap rabbits, or just any rabbit you find for sale along a country road. That goes for rabbits of breeds other than the New Zealand White or the Florida White, of course, but rabbits of the same breed from different rabbitries often vary greatly in their ability to perform.

The fact, as has been pointed out, is that New Zealands and Floridas are among the most consistent high-performance rabbits of any breed. Within these breeds, however, you must obtain rabbits that have a history of performing up to the expectations you have for them. Therefore, the best possible person from whom to obtain your rabbits is that rabbit raiser whose animals are performing precisely as you would like yours to do.

How to Find Them

You are not the first person in the world to look for them. Others have gone before you and it's up to you to follow. And it's easy, with just a little detective work. Here are some leads to get you started.

First, visit your local feed and farm supply store. If you don't know where it is, check the yellow pages of the phone book for a listing under Farm Supply, Animal Feed, or Hay and Grain Dealers. Ten to one you will find yours on "Railroad Ave-

New Zealand White doe and litter.

nue" or "Depot Street" or some such similar address next to the railroad tracks because grain and other supplies often are delivered in boxcars.

Tell the dealer you plan to raise rabbits for your table and you seek outstanding breeding stock from one of his feed customers who is adept at doing what you intend to do. Don't be bashful about this. The dealer will be glad to try to help. For one thing, farm supply store people are just about as friendly and candid as any you will find anywhere. They are well-trained and interested store personnel who really love their work. For another, they are always looking for new rabbit feed customers—and you have the potential to be one of the best! Rabbit feed sales are important to these stores. In fact, rabbit feed sales are one of the fastest-growing aspects of their business. Major milling companies agree on this. For several such companies, no feed type is selling faster. Rabbits are becoming extremely popular for the very reason that you have in mind: meat on your table—and excellent, high-quality meat at that.

Find Best Breeders

Get the names of a few recommended breeders—at least three or four. The dealer's customers are looking for customers too. Phone your prospects and explain what you have in mind. State your **goal**. If they indicate that they have rabbits with a history of and potential for performing as you wish them to, make an appointment to visit the rabbitry. You should visit three or four before you make up your mind from whom to buy.

Questions to Ask

It's a good idea to write down your questions before you make such a visit, and to ask the same questions at each place you visit.

Here are some things to ask:

1. How long have you been raising rabbits?
2. How long have you been raising New Zealand Whites or Florida Whites?
3. Do you keep production records and will you show them to me? (These should include hutch cards with litter history.)
4. What and how much do you feed your rabbits?
5. Are the rabbits pedigreed (does the breeder keep written records of ancestry for each rabbit)?
6. Do you tattoo numbers in the rabbits' ears?
7. Do you ever exhibit your rabbits at a show?
8. Will you take the rabbits back and refund my money if I am not happy with them?
9. Are you willing to answer questions, perhaps over the phone or during a visit some evening or weekend?
10. How much do you charge?

You may have more questions, but these are among the most important. A good breeder should be happy to answer them all satisfactorily for you. Let's look at the best possible answers:

1. He has been raising rabbits for several years at least. He is not a novice and is not a child. Learning successful rabbit raising takes time. I'd look for experience of the rabbit raiser when I look for breeding rabbits. I've had more than one 4-H leader crit-

icize me for this approach, and, in fact, I raised rabbits for sale myself as a boy. But you are buying the experience of the rabbit producer as much as the rabbits themselves. That's not to say that a youngster can't produce outstanding rabbits. But if you want to improve your chances of getting the best rabbits, buy them from the experienced breeder.

2. The above goes also for this question. You need to buy from someone who has experience producing your chosen breed.

3. Each breeding rabbit should have a hutch card, as shown in the illustration. From it you can tell if the rabbit (whether male or female) is producing youngsters regularly and of good size and health. Some breeders keep stock record books as well, although for efficiency and simplicity they may wish to confine their record keeping to the hutch cards. In any event, the breeder should be willing to share this information with you. Remember that not every rabbit in his herd is going to produce every time, on schedule, without missing a beat. That simply is not realistic. But you should take note of performance and compare it to that of other rabbit raisers you will visit.

HUTCH RECORD

Name _Georgetown Miss_ Ear No. _BB 993_
Hutch No. _____ Breed_FLORIDA White_ Registry No. _____
Birth Date _9/9/83_ Sire_BBA52_ Dam_BBC62_

BUCK	DATE SERVED	DATE TESTED	DATE KINDLED	NO. BORN	WEIGHT		WEANING		LITTER MARK	REMARKS
					21 d	56 d	NO.	AGE		
BB433	3/3/84		4/3/84	7			7	8 wks		4 Bucks, 3 Does

Hutch card.

4. The breeder should be feeding rabbit pellets as the foundation of his herd's diet. He may be supplementing the pellets with additional feeds, and he should be willing to tell you about them. He should know how much he is feeding his rabbits and how much it costs him. At worst he should be keeping records of his feed costs and each rabbit's consumption. At best he should be able to tell you the feed/meat conversion ratio of his herd and it should be in the 4:1 range (4 pounds of feed to 1 pound of live weight rabbit at slaughter).

Rabbit Registration
Certificate of Entry in the Stud Book of
AMERICAN RABBIT BREEDERS ASSOCIATION, INCORPORATED

No. 1573 G

NAME	Sweet Son	EAR NO. BB6D	BREED Tan		SEX Buck	COLOR Chocolate

BORN 7-25-72   WEIGHT 4½   WINNINGS 1st Jr. Buck (8), B.O.S. (50) BOSV (5) Montco RBA 1973, Fairfield Co. RBA 1973, Green Mt. RBA 1973   DATE REG. 11-23-73

NAME OF BREEDER Robert Bennett   ADDRESS 624 Lawlins Road Wyckoff, N. J.

PURCHASED FROM   ADDRESS

REGISTRAR'S NAME Charles Lyons   ADDRESS Rutland, Vermont

DESCRIPTION: TYPE Very good (compact)   BONE Medium   COLOR Very Good   BODY Very Good   FUR Good fly-back & texture

HEAD Full   EARS Length 3½"   EYES Clear   CONDITION Very Good   BALANCE Good

REG. REMARKS Very nice chocolate tan, very good markings.

OWNER Robert Bennett   STREET 624 Lawlins Road   TOWN Wyckoff,   STATE New Jersey

DATE FILED 12-5-73

			G. G. SIRE In England	REG. NO.
			COLOR	WT.
			GRAND CHAMPION NO.	
SIRE Sir Brian REG. NO. 424C	GR. SIRE English Import REG. NO.		G. G. DAM In England	REG. NO.
COLOR Lilac WT. 4½	COLOR K.B. 70 Lilac WT. 5		COLOR	WT.
GRAND CHAMPION NO.	GRAND CHAMPION NO.		GRAND CHAMPION NO.	
			G. G. SIRE Buckeye Lad	REG. NO.
			COLOR Lilac	WT. 5
	GR. DAM Harriet REG. NO. 433C		GRAND CHAMPION NO.	
	COLOR Chocolate WT. 4½		G. G. DAM Prioress of Kirklees	REG. NO. 1267B
	GRAND CHAMPION NO.		COLOR Chocolate	WT. 5½
			GRAND CHAMPION NO.	
			G. G. SIRE Sir Ralph	REG. NO. 2027B
			COLOR Chocolate	WT. 4½
DAM Bittersweet REG. NO. 3997E	GR. SIRE Shers' Man REG. NO.		GRAND CHAMPION NO.	
COLOR Chocolate WT. 4½	COLOR Chocolate WT. 4½		G. G. DAM Mary L.	REG. NO.
GRAND CHAMPION NO.	GRAND CHAMPION NO.		COLOR Chocolate	WT. 4½
			GRAND CHAMPION NO.	
			G. G. SIRE Sir Ralph	REG. NO. 2027B
	GR. DAM Dack-Me-Jo REG. NO.		COLOR Chocolate	WT. 4½
	COLOR Chocolate WT. 4		GRAND CHAMPION NO.	
	GRAND CHAMPION NO.		G. G. DAM Lady Clara	REG. NO. 974C
			COLOR Chocolate	WT. 5½
			GRAND CHAMPION NO.	

Edward Peck

Secretary

Registration certificate.

Written Records

5. The breeder should keep a written record of the ancestry of every rabbit he owns and he should supply you with a pedigree certificate showing at least three generations of ancestry of the rabbit you take home. Why?

First, understand that a pedigree is merely a written record of ancestry, and it is only as accurate as the person who writes it. Most of all, it means that the owner keeps track of his rabbits, knows which one is which, and mates only those pairs that he consciously wishes to mate. This is a careful breeder who **selects** the parents of each new generation. He is much more likely to produce good rabbits than the breeder who pays no attention to who's who and allows indiscriminate mating to take place. We'll go into breeding techniques, including selection, in a later chapter, but in the meantime insist upon pedigreed rabbits. While we are on this point, you may be wondering about "registered" rabbits and whether they are the same as "pedigreed."

Registered rabbits are adult pedigreed rabbits of certain purebred breeds recognized by the American Rabbit Breeders Association, Inc., which maintains "stud" or registration records at its headquarters in Illinois. A licensed registrar examines an adult pedigreed rabbit to ascertain whether it qualifies for registration by the association. If it does, it signifies that the rabbit meets the **minimum** requirements for the breed as outlined by the association. We'll get into that more later.

If a rabbit raiser who produces breeding stock for sale keeps his breeders registered as a regular practice, you are assured, better than any other way, that the animals he produces meet at least the minimum requirements for the breed. In the case of New Zealands and Florida Whites, these requirements relate to the rabbits' ability to produce a meaty carcass, which is, of course, what you will be trying to do. Pedigreed, better yet, registered rabbits are your very best assurance that you will get in subsequent litters high-quality specimens that resemble their parents.

Of course, registered rabbits are purebred. It is possible to undertake your rabbit project with crossbreds or hybrids (and in fact it may be highly desirable, as has been stated), but the availability of such rabbits that can perform up to your expectations is likely to be limited. Crossbred rabbits cannot be registered, but detailed pedigree records should be kept nevertheless.

Tan rabbit being tattooed.

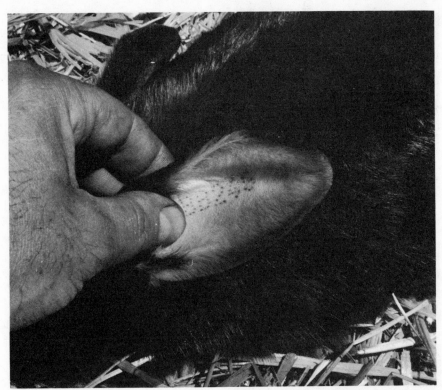

Private ear number in left ear.

6. Look for a number or letters or a combination of the two in the left ear of each breeding rabbit. Such identification is essential to keep track of individuals. A selective breeding program cannot be carried out if you don't know which rabbit is which. Each pedigree should carry the rabbit's number or letter designation. The right ear is used for the registration number, which is applied by the registrar upon successful completion of his examination of each rabbit he deems worthy of registration by the American Rabbit Breeders Association.

The three rabbits you take home should have identification numbers, but it will not be necessary for you to earmark any of their offspring that are destined for the table. Later on you will want to replace your original breeders, and when you do the replacements should be marked. You need not purchase tattooing equipment because you can have the tattooing done for you, as I will explain.

New Zealand Whites on judging table.

Shows Are Important

7. Why should you care whether a meat rabbit goes to a show and wins a ribbon or a trophy? Will a fancy rosette in the past make your meal any tastier in the future? Quite possibly.

Rabbits are judged at rabbit shows according to a point system as well as by comparison to other rabbits there. In the case of New Zealand Whites and Floridas, most of the points are allotted to body type, or conformation, and those that win the most points are those carrying the most meat in the right places. If the breeder from whom you buy attends shows at least occasionally, and if he has won a few ribbons, the judges have ruled that the rabbits are built right—to produce meat. It is highly likely that the breeder with pedigreed, registered rabbits that go to shows is one who raises rabbits that will produce the results you are after.

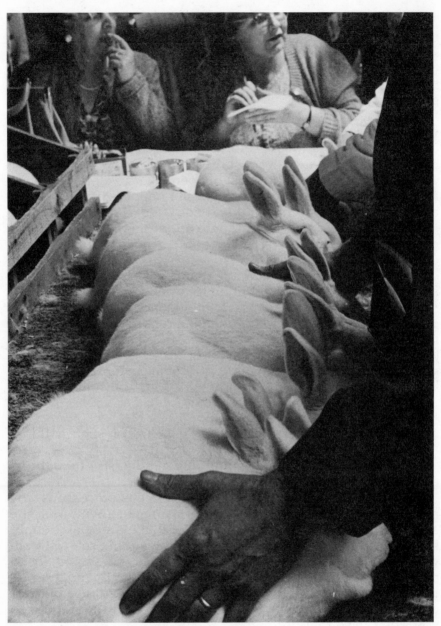

New Zealand Whites on judging table.

8. Now you‘are getting down to business. Does the breeder stand behind his rabbits? He does if he guarantees your satisfaction or another rabbit. It should be pointed out that selling breeding stock to beginners is not without hazard. I have been doing it for years, and I have refunded some money and replaced some rabbits.

No question about it, some rabbits from the best breeders with the best ancestry may nevertheless turn out to be, well, duds. They up and die for no apparent reason. Or they don't grow properly or they won't breed readily or if they do they won't take care of their litters. It happens. With well-bred rabbits from well-managed rabbitries it doesn't happen often, it's true, but it does happen. That said and admitted, it is also true that many beginners don't take proper care of their newly acquired charges, either because of negligence, or, much more likely, because of ignorance.

Let me give you an example that proves to my satisfaction at least that there's no accounting for what some people will do.

A young man of apparent intelligence, a recent college graduate, took home a trio of breeding rabbits along with typed instructions for their feeding. The instructions were quite explicit: pellets, water, hay. Perhaps some dry bread but no greens (the rabbits were young and unaccustomed to them). Nothing else. Period. Clear? Simple? You might think so.

Two weeks later came the phone call:

"Why is my rabbit throwing up?"

This was new—the first time I'd heard of such a thing. "What did you feed it?"

"Well, it was a rainy day, and quite chilly, so I thought I'd give it some chicken soup."

Actually, there are many more or less absurd reasons why rabbits don't perform because of mismanagement, but the seller of breeding stock must remember that his stock is bought for breeding. He must be willing to follow up his sale with advice, with guidance. And if things go awry, he should try to make them right. Improper feeding is probably the biggest reason rabbits don't perform as wished, with overfeeding a big part of the problem. Later on we will cover feeding thoroughly so you won't have that problem.

Replacement Pays

More than one seller of breeding stock knows that the occasional replacement of a breeding rabbit for an unhappy customer can be one of the biggest sales tools. The word gets around when somebody treats you more than fairly. So the seller should be willing to bend over backwards to please you. Or he shouldn't be selling breeding stock (or, maybe he hasn't been selling much of it, which is a good reason not to become his customer in the first place.)

9. We've just about covered this one—the aftermarket advice. The seller of breeding stock should not mind your questions and planned, mutually convenient visits.

10. What will you pay for these rabbits? It will depend upon a number of considerations, including the ages of the rabbits.

If you buy rabbits 6–8 months of age, you will pay top price. That's because the breeder has kept these rabbits that long, provided each with its own hutch, and quite probably considered them future breeders of his own. They are likely to be the most promising of all his rabbits and valued accordingly. He would not have kept them this long, most probably, if he didn't think highly of them.

Just-weaned rabbits will cost you the least and may well be your best buy. Not just because of what you will pay but because they will give you time to become accustomed to them before they go into service as breeders. Rabbits 2 to 3 months old will be ready for breeding in another 2 to 4 months, depending upon the breed. Depending upon the time of year and their availability, I might make them my number one recommendation.

On the other side, you might get the breeder to part with does about 2 years old. These could be an excellent choice at a lower price than for those prime 6–8 monthers. If a breeder has kept a rabbit for a couple of years, you can be sure that it has proved itself to be a fine rabbit; otherwise he would not have kept it that long. On the other hand, its potential as a producer definitely is limited. The breeder may have obtained offspring from it that he has kept, and he may wish to make room in his rabbitry for them. Under these conditions he may well be willing to part with the rabbit at a reduced price.

A doe at 2 years of age still has a year or more of breeding life. A buck is good for another 4 or 5 or more—up to 7 or 8 years of age in many instances.

If your producer of breeding stock keeps rabbits, particularly does, of this age or even longer, he may get nothing for them later. You might do well to buy one of these 2-year-old does, mated to one of his bucks, and also a younger doe and buck, recently weaned. That way you will have a litter on the way, a pair growing up, and the buck ready to mate with the older doe after her upcoming litter is weaned.

Prices

How much should you pay? The youngest rabbits should cost no more than $10–$20 each, and more likely closer to $10. The older doe shouldn't cost any more, while if you bought the 6–8-month rabbits, they would have cost you $30 or more each.

Some rabbits will cost a lot more. Show winners and show prospects from a top show herd are in that category. Dont' buy these rabbits unless you plan to show. Overall, you ought to be able to get your three rabbits for a total of no more than $45— that's the most I'd pay for rabbits geared to home meat production on a limited basis.

You might even pay nothing. It's possible that the breeder is overstocked, or, in the fall, has more rabbits than he wants to carry over through the winter.

In northern areas of the country, some airlines forbid winter shipments. Many breeding stock producers conduct a mail order business with air shipments and are confined to local sales in the winter. They may have too many rabbits on hand.

At the same time, they may hate to reduce their inventory by filling their freezer. That's because these rabbits in their over-supply may be viewed as having good breeding potential. A breeder may let you have some of them if you agree to let him have the pick of the litter or several offspring in return. You won't really know the answer to this question unless you ask it. When you come right down to it, the name of the game is to put high-quality meat on your table at low cost, so this is no time to be bashful. It is a time to be inquisitive, imaginative, and unafraid to suggest an innovative arrangement. You have nothing to lose, and money and rabbits to gain.

Chapter 4

Selecting Your Rabbits

After you have identified the breeder from whom you will make your purchase, how will you select the rabbits you will take home? The following should guide you in your selection. First, let's make some generalizations that apply to both New Zealands and Florida Whites. Then, let's look at the individual breeds.

Your rabbits must be alert and active. Inquisitive. They should come to the front of the cage when you open the door. Watch out for any that look listless and hang back. Look for a bright eye and a dry nose. Check the front paws. The insides of the front paws would be matted if the rabbit had a cold and wiped its nose. Look under the hutch. The droppings that fall through the wire mesh floor should be hard and round. If not, the rabbit may have diarrhea. Pick up the rabbit. It should be clean all over. Look at the footpads. They should be clean, dry, and well-furred. Look into the ears. They should be clean.

Put the rabbit on a flat surface on which it can stand easily. A table, shelf, or box covered with carpet or burlap gives it a firm footing. Gently stroke the fur from the rump toward the head, against the "grain." It should roll back or snap back to its original position. It should be thick and springy.

Good safe way to carry a rabbit.

Check Teeth

Check the teeth. Upper front teeth should barely overlap the tips of the lower front teeth for a slight scissors effect when chewing. Beware of teeth that overlap too much. Rabbit's teeth grow throughout their lives and malocclusion can cause permanent difficulty in eating and, in fact, eventual death by starvation. Make sure legs are straight—neither bowed in or out. Feel the rabbit all over, top and bottom. It should be smooth and plump, with no cuts, abrasions, or abscesses.

Now let's take a look at what the two breeds should be like.

Florida White

Here's a rather short rabbit with well developed shoulders and hindquarters. Very compact and solid. You can barely pick up a good one with one hand. The depth or height of the body should be about the same as the width. The hindquarters should be smooth and round. The loin should be firm and meaty, as should be the ribsection and the shoulders, with the shoulders slightly narrower than the rump. The neck should be barely noticeable. An adult should weigh about 5 pounds, no less than 4 and no more than 6. A 5-pound ball of fur-covered meat is what you seek.

Florida White.

Prize-winning New Zealand White and owner.

New Zealand White

The New Zealand White exhibits the same physique as the Florida, except that it is twice as big, and thus a little less round, a little longer. It should have the same well-knit, broad, smooth appearance to be firm and meaty. Full-grown or senior does should weigh 10–12 pounds. Senior bucks, 8 months of age or older, should weigh 9–11 pounds.

For more specific descriptions of both breeds, and others as well, consult the **Standard of Perfection**, which is a book published by the American Rabbit Breeders Association that contains all the details on all the breeds it recognizes. In the back of this book I tell you how to get a copy.

As a beginner, your ability to recognize the best specimens available of either breed is limited by your inexperience in looking them over. Even with the tips in this book and the precise specifications in the **Standard of Perfection**, you are going to be somewhat at the mercy of the seller. That's why it's so important to make every effort to identify a breeder who is reaching the goal you have in mind. He can't have very many poor rabbits if he's being successful now at what you have in mind for your own future.

Chapter 5

The Second Key to Success: The Right Housing and Equipment

How you house your rabbits will mean the difference between their life and death, your success or failure. While it's true that rabbits will survive in a variety of habitats for awhile, it is courting disaster to confine them to housing that is anything less than functional, efficient, and yes, even attractive.

I said **confine** them. That's how rabbits are raised successfully. In confinement. It is also the way most poultry and hogs are raised these days, but rabbits have been raised in confinement for many more years than other species.

Years ago in Europe rabbits were given free run of the barn that housed the other species. They did not run away because they lived off the feed given to the larger animals. Because they were free to run and burrow where they wished, their owner had practically no control over when and with whom they mated. When he wanted a rabbit dinner he had a real challenge in catching it. When he caught it he often was surprised by what he got. With no control over feeding and mating the result was often tough, stringy, bony fare. Rabbits' reputations were not enhanced by this lifestyle.

Some rabbit raisers tried confining them to large pens, perhaps 20 feet square or larger, called colonies. Colony raising is an improvement over the run-of-the-barn method, but it still doesn't measure up to confinement in individual pens, or hutches.

All-wire hutches used inside a building.

Wire-Mesh Box

I recommend hutches that are protected from the elements for the good of the rabbits and the rabbit keeper. Each adult rabbit will require its own hutch, which is a wire-mesh box. All of these hutches will need to be under some sort of roof for protection from sun, snow, and rain. Sidewalls will be needed in most rabbitries, at least for part of the year. A roof that covers the rabbit keeper will allow him to spend more time with his charges during bad weather. It is not important to keep rabbits warm, so long as they are kept dry and out of the wind. It is very important to keep them well-ventilated and clean. That's what wire-mesh hutches do best.

If you keep rabbits in anything other than wire-mesh hutches, you are asking for trouble. They will gnaw wood and soak it with urine. They will be smelly until they escape or die. Die? Certainly, because dampness from urine causes all kinds of health problems. Wire-mesh hutches eliminate damp floors and keep your rabbits healthy.

New Zealand Whites in wire hutches in building.

All-wire hutches in building.

Let's suppose you put rabbits in a packing crate pen, which has happened more times than it should. You sprinkle some shavings on the wooden floor. The rabbits urinate and the bedding becomes wet. They add a little manure. Even if you clean this out daily, your rabbits will very likely soon contract intestinal worms, ear mites, ulcerated feet, weepy eyes from ammonia fumes, and most likely colds from the generally damp condition. I almost forgot abscesses. And wry neck.

For the rabbit, this is really grim. For you, it's almost as bad. What you have created is an eyesore that offends the nose as well. Furthermore, it is likely to offend your spouse or other family members. That could be enough to put you out of business. If it isn't, consider the neighbors. And the local health officer. I'll bet anything he will be called soon. That **will** put you out of business. It's a darn good thing, too, and I hope it happens soon enough to save the rabbits, which will doubtless take up residence at the local humane society animal shelter if they live that long.

So there is no question about it. Unless you put your rabbits in self-cleaning, completely ventilated all-wire hutches, you may just as well not have rabbits at all. If you follow my advice they will be clean, virtually odor-free, healthy, and beautiful as well as productive and profitable. In addition, an arrangement of all-wire hutches offers unmatched efficiency because you can feed and water your charges without so much as opening the hutch doors.

Shelter Needed

Your best bet is to arrange the hutches in a single tier inside a barn, shed, garage, or specially built structure. They can be installed outdoors under a roof with "legs" like a table with a slanting top. If so, you will need to fence them in to protect them from dogs, cats, and curious children.

I haven't always had a barn for my rabbits, but I do think that's the best place for hutches. Mine have been inside a barn only since 1980. Because I think it is so important for you to get a sense of the absolute need for all-wire hutches under some kind of structure for protection from the weather, I'm going to describe the rabbitries I've had myself, and what I learned from building and using them. It will give you a good idea, I think, why I now have all-wire hutches hanging from the joists of a barn.

Back in 1948 welded wire was not generally available, to my knowledge. As a 12-year-old I began with two wood and wire hutches beneath a sunporch. The hutches were basically wooden boxes, but with hardware cloth floors and chicken wire fronts. Neither hardware cloth nor chicken wire has the rigidity of welded wire and, therefore, needs wood framing members. Rabbits can, I found, chew right through chicken wire, given a little time to practice. My first pair of rabbits, New Zealand Reds, nevertheless produced several litters in those first hutches.

Soon I decided I would need more room and I moved the hutches to a wooded area across the tiny brook that ran about 50 feet behind the house. We owned eight acres, wooded and open, on Mendon Mountain in Vermont. You reached the rabbitry area via a wooden footbridge I made by cutting logs and poles and nailing and lashing them together. In the woods, adjacent to an open garden we had carved out of the forest, I built about a dozen wood and wire hutches. The fronts and floors were wire like the first two; the rest were made of scrap lumber covered with tarpaper and rolled roofing. I added six more hutches that I converted from mink cages given to me by a new neighbor who bought a place that once included a mink farm.

I arranged these hutches in a single tier on scrap lumber legs, in two facing rows with a 3-foot aisle with one hutch on the end as a cap. I made a gate on the other end. I nailed chicken wire to the rear legs of the hutches, all around, to keep out dogs and other animals. On especially cold or rainy days I unrolled feed sacks tacked to the tops of the hutches, as storm curtains. This configuration gave the rabbits considerable protection.

Ramshackle Shelter

While it is true that this rabbitry worked fairly well (and the key to its success was the hardware cloth floors), it was a sight to behold. Ramshackle was what my mother called it. Of course, it was set in the woods on a mountain in Vermont, where the nearest neighbor was a quarter of a mile away (and you should have seen his chicken coop and dog kennel). During bad weather I didn't spend much time with the rabbits, and the looks of it aside, it really was not functionally ideal. Today, 35 years later, I still see this sort of backyard arrangement and it is quite an eyesore. You might get away with it in the woods on a mountain top.

Author with one of prior rabbitry sheds in background.

Interior of shed in photo above.

Years later, in New Jersey, I had a small shed, about 12 feet square, completely enclosed, with a window and a door and a concrete floor. It was used primarily for a workshop and garden tool storage. It became the site of my second rabbitry.

I built six all-wire hutches, each 2½ by 3 feet by 18 inches high. I hung them on S-hooks, three tiers high, to a wooden framework made of 2" × 2" lumber, on casters. Under each hutch I installed a sloping galvanized dropping board backed up by 3-foot lengths of aluminum eavestrough with end caps to catch the droppings and urine. I emptied the eavestroughs each night. The recipients were azaleas, rosebushes, pachysandra, and dogwood trees, plus an assortment of evergreen shrubs and flowers. The lot was too shady for vegetables.

This tiny rabbitry was all I had room for but it met my objectives perfectly by supplying meat for the table and a limited amount of breeding stock for sale. The storage shed was easy to ventilate. It was cool in the summer, being shaded by tall oak trees. It had no heat in winter but that was fine. I kept the window open all year. I built the hutches for about $5 each (they would be $10 in 1984), and the framework of 2×2s, dropping boards, eavestroughs, hardware, and casters came to about $30. This setup would have worked as well in a garage. I kept two bucks and two does and had two holding pens. I remember this arrangement fondly.

By 1970, however, my family had grown. The three-bedroom cape on the quarter-acre lot wouldn't accommodate us all in lots of ways. So we bought a bigger place on a bigger lot in the same town. The backyard was large, partially wooded and quite secluded. At the same time, I was experiencing a greater demand for my rabbits, having attained some notable victories at the shows in the Mid-Atlantic and New England states. So I decided to build a bigger rabbitry.

Storage Shed

I bought prefabricated steel sections to build a storage shed 20 feet long by 4 feet deep, about 7 feed high in the front (which was open) and 5 feet high in the back (which was enclosed). In this shed I arranged two tiers of all-wire hutches. The top tier consisted of 2½ by 3-foot hutches for does, hung from the roof. The hutches on the bottom were only 1½ feet deep by 3 feet wide, fine for bucks and young stock. They were all-wire but

Tarpaulin is rolled down on outside shed on stormy days.

were supported by 2-foot wooden legs made from 1 x 2-inch lumber. A galvanized sheet metal dropping board under the top tier sent the manure and urine to the ground below and behind the lower tier. Droppings from the lower tier went directly to the ground. I placed a sheet of linoleum on the top of the bottom tier to form a shelf I used for examining the rabbits and for such operations as tattooing and weighing. I shaded the front of this 3 x 20 shed with a tarpaulin. On stormy days I tied it down to keep out rain or snow.

Outdoor use of wire hutches in a shed.

More Hutches

A year later, experiencing even greater demand than the six large (doe) hutches and six smaller hutches could meet, I put up another 3 × 20 shed, identical to the first, 3 feet away and facing it. I hung nine 2 × 2½-foot doe hutches (sufficient in size for the small breed I was raising) and a dozen buck hutches in the new section. I roofed the center aisle with corrugated white fiberglass that admitted light and reflected the heat of the sun. The aisle roof was a foot higher than the roofs of the sheds, which allowed for plenty of ventilation. I put a screen door on each end. An automatic watering system was a final touch. For 6 years this rabbitry produced hundreds of rabbits for sale annually.

Even though the shed was galvanized and then painted with three coats of anti-rust epoxy paint, it soon began to rust, and I vowed then never to place hutches against walls. Not just against walls of metal but any kind. It is impossible to keep metal from rusting and impossible to keep anything else clean. When I built my barn several years later I maintained a 4-foot aisle between the hutches and the walls.

Another thing I learned is to hang the hutches from the roof of the building. It is impractical to stand them on legs. With legs in the way, cleaning is quite a chore. But it is no problem with no obstructions.

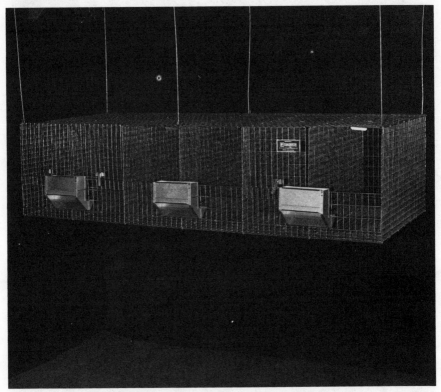

Wire hutches suspended by wire from joists of barn.

Wire hutches can be hung in tiers from joists.

Hang From Joists

That's why the 36 hutches I now have in my barn are hanging from the joists from lengths of 12½ gauge wire. The hutches hang in two tiers. The dropping board under the top tier is made of corrugated fiberglass, which won't rust like the galvanized sheet metal did. I keep a small piece of the fiberglass handy to use occasionally as a scraper. It fits the grooves perfectly. Once a week, usually on a Saturday morning, I scrape off the dropping boards. Only twice a year, in early spring and late fall, do I fork out the manure underneath, for the benefit of the garden. Some of it goes in the compost heap for use in future planting. I can always use it because I am always planting trees, shrubs, and flowers as well as vegetables.

My hutches hang back-to-back. They occupy a space 18 feet long and 5 feet wide, but with room between them and the walls, they take up about half of a building that is 24 feet square, about the size of a two-car garage. In fact, my "barn" is built from the plans for my garage and a rabbitry like mine could go into just about any garage. My barn does have a gravel floor over a couple of feet of sand, which is one reason why I can let the droppings sit there six months at a time. I have no drainage problem at all. With a concrete floor more frequent cleaning would be necessary.

It seems these days you can find almost anything in the garage but the car, and many rabbitries are found there. Rabbitries in shed extensions to the back of a garage are common. So are rabbitries in garden sheds and other storage buildings.

Ventilation Important

The most important consideration when housing your rabbits in a building is ventilation. Keep windows open. Add a gable vent if you don't have one. An exhaust fan may be required in some climates during the summer months.

Let's suppose, however, you don't have a suitable building. You can still have a suitable rabbitry. Years ago, when we built hutches of wood and wire, each hutch was its own building. It had a wooden roof and sides, and it stood on four legs. A collection of these, as I have related, is not attractive. Besides being ugly, they were expensive and labor-intensive to build. The approach to take these days is to put up a pole shed that covers the total number of hutches you plan to have, and hang the hutches inside. You can enclose the sides of this shed with wire fencing

Commercially made stacking hutches.

and plant and train vines to climb it. You can hang fiberglass or plywood panels over this for winter. A large overhang to the roof will keep things shady and dry. Depending on how elaborate you want to build this shed, it can have a door that will admit you, and can be locked. If you can't build it large enough for you, put a fence all the way around it, about 4 feet away. Plant shrubs or flowers around the fence.

An alternative to pole construction, which is a lot like setting fence posts and then roofing them over, is the railroad tie foundation. Set heavy creosoted railroad ties or large pressure-treated landscaping timbers on a sand or gravel base. Nail a 2 × 4 plate to them and use regular stud construction techniques from there up. Such a foundation is not usually considered permanent by municipal officials, and won't drive your taxes up.

I hope I have convinced you that the all-wire hutch, well-protected from the weather and intruders, is the only way to go. I don't know what else I can tell you except that the wire hutch actually is cheaper and easier to build than one made of wood and wire. So you are going to have healthy rabbits, a good looking rabbitry and even lower costs if you follow my advice. What's left is to tell you how to build these hutches.

First, however, you must decide how many you want. If you plan only a family meat project, I urge you to purchase the two or three hutches you desire from your local feed dealer or from a mailorder supplier. Building your own makes economic sense only if you plan to build ten hutches or more. If you buy, you can expect to pay about $10 each for a basic hutch. Some come with legs and dropping pans and they will run you up to $25 each.

How to Build

If you plan to build your own, here's what you need:

TOOLS

A pair of wire-cutting pliers.
A pair of slip-joint pliers.
A tape measure.
A hammer.
A pair of J-clip pliers. Get them from a farm supply store or a supplier listed in this book.
A 3- or 4-foot length of 2 x 4 lumber.

MATERIALS

1 x 2-inch welded wire fencing, 14 gauge.
½ x 1-inch welded wire, 14 or 16 gauge.
J-clips. Get them where you get the J-clip pliers.
Door latches.
Door hangers.

You will need welded wire fencing in both 14-gauge 1 x 2-inch and ½ x 1-inch, or 16 gauge ½ x 1-inch, with the 14-gauge wire being heavier, better, more expensive, and more difficult to obtain in many areas.

Welded wire comes in two types—galvanized **before** welding and galvanized **after** welding. The latter costs more but is more rigid and lasts longer. Welded wire wears out by oxidation and wire that is galvanized after welding has more material to oxidize. It appears thicker, especially at the joints, than wire galvanized before welding, which is smoother to the touch. You can build with wire galvanized before welding but the hutches will not last as long, nor be as rigid. I have used both kinds. Galvanized-after is superior.

Some have experimented with vinyl-covered welded wire, but rabbits love to gnaw and easily can strip the vinyl covering from the wire, which soon will rust.

Another point: there are both **1 x 2**-inch wire and **2 x 1**-inch wire. The former has wires every inch of the **width** of the roll. The 1 x 2-inch is better, but 2 x 1 will work. When calculating dimensions, keep in mind that you lose an inch—or two— each time you cut this wire.

Buy Latches, Hangers

Door latches are so inexpensive that buying them is a better use of time than making them unless you are good at metal working and have a supply of bolts or rivets and a riveter. The same can be said for the door hangers.

All-wire rabbit hutches are simply boxes with 1 x 2 wire on front, back, top, and sides, and ½ x 1 wire on the bottom.

Overall dimensions of hutches are up to you, as they can be made in just about any size up to maximum widths of available wire, but there are three considerations regarding size:

1. Provide nearly a square foot of floor space per pound of adult doe. A 2½-foot by 3-foot hutch will accommodate a medium (New Zealand) size breed doe and her litter to weaning time. This size is fine for smaller breeds as well, and many raisers who have no intention of raising giant breeds but do plan to try the smaller sizes build only the 30 x 36-inch hutch. On the other hand, to conserve space and materials, you may build hutches that are 24 x 30 inches for small breeds such as Florida Whites. A 24 x 30 hutch will also serve as a New Zealand buck's hutch.

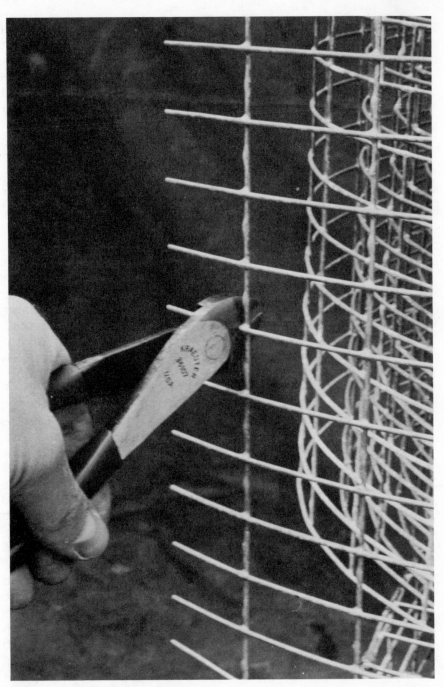

Cutting stubs of wire flush.

An 18 × 30 hutch will house a small breed buck. A buck can use more space for exercise, however, and it is not extravagant to build all your hutches large enough to accommodate does and litters of the size breed you choose. Not only will you have extra space for your bucks, you will have total flexibility and will be able to move rabbits from one hutch to another without worrying whether the size is right.

2. Depth front to back should not exceed 2½ feet or you won't be able to reach rabbits in the rear. Height should be 16 or 18 inches.

3. If you are going to build hutches to fit inside a building, tailor the sizes within the above two guidelines. Wire comes in widths 12 inches to 72 inches in 6-inch increments.

30 Inches × 36 Inches for Medium Breeds

Buy 100 feet of 1 × 2 wire 36 inches wide. Buy either 26 feet of ½ × 1 wire 36 inches wide or 31 feet of ½ × 1 wire 30 inches wide. If you plan to build all-wire nest boxes, as described later, you will need more of the ½ × 1 wire, so plan and buy accordingly. Buy 2 pounds of J-clips. There are about 450 to the pound. Each hutch takes about 90 clips and you will bend a few out of shape as you learn to work with them.

From the roll of 1 × 2 wire cut a piece 62 inches long. Cut it flush and while you're at it, cut the stubs off flush from the rest of the roll. Lay the piece on the floor so it curls down (humps up). Stand on one end and gently bend the other toward you, moving your feet forward as necessary to flatten the wire. Take care not to kink it; simply reverse the curve with enough pressure to take the bend of the roll out of it. Turn it over. This is important so, in the next steps, you don't bend against the welded joints, but with them. Most rolls of wire come with the one-inch wires on top of the 2-inch wires as you view the roll before unrolling. If you should obtain wire rolled the opposite way, then note it and do not bend against the welds.

With the wire on the floor, measure 16 inches from one end and lay your 2 × 4 board across it at that point. Stand on the 2 × 4 and gently pull the 16-inch section toward you. Hold it vertically. Reach down with your hammer and gently strike each strand of wire against the 2 × 4 to fix the 90° angle. Measure 16 inches from the other end and repeat the process of bending. You have just formed the front, the back, and the top. Set it aside.

Bending hutch wire corners around vertical post.

Cut 30 inches more off the roll and flatten the resulting 30-inch by 36-inch piece as above. Cut it flush and cut the stubs flush off the roll. As you cut, notice that a slight flick of the wrist down and away from the welds will snap the wire off cleanly with little effort. Measure 16 inches up (you are splitting the piece) and cut off flush. The remaining piece will be 30 inches by 18 inches (plus stubs). Measure 16 inches down it and cut off 2 inches (plus stubs). The 2-inch "waste" strip will be from the center. You will use it later, so set it aside. You now have the sides of your hutch.

Bending hutch wire corners with 2 × 4.

If you bought 36-inch-wide $\frac{1}{2} \times 1$ wire, cut off 30 inches flush and cut the stubs off the roll. If you bought 30-inch wire, cut off 36 inches. Do not flatten this piece of floor wire, which curves or humps up with the $\frac{1}{2}$-inch wires up, unless it has an extreme curl, perhaps if it is cut from the center of the roll, where it is curled tighter. The idea is to have the $\frac{1}{2}$-inch wires uppermost, to provide a smoother surface for the rabbits and to keep an upward spring so that it won't sag from the weight of the rabbits.

How to Assemble

Now you are ready to assemble the hutch, as you have cut out all the pieces except for the door and some more 2-inch strips that you will clip later to the four sides near the floor as a "baby saver" feature. More about that later.

Using J-clips and the J-clip pliers, fasten the top, front, and back sections (the 16×30 sections) to the side sections. Use a J-clip every 4 inches, starting with the corners. Make sure the vertical 1-inch wires are on the outside of the hutch. That way you will have horizontal wires on the inside where they will make neat, tight corners when fastened to the end-top-end section. After a little practice you will find that squeezing on the J-clips requires another little flip of the wrist or a second squeeze to assure the tightest grip of the clip.

After clipping together the front and back and ends and top, turn the hutch on its top and lay the floor wire on it, with the curve and the $\frac{1}{2}$-inch wires down, or toward the top of the hutch, remembering that those wires provide the smoother floor and that an upward spring will result from this position to prevent floor sag.

Clip the floor wire on, starting in one corner, using clips every 4 inches. If the fit is too tight in a corner, which can happen if the 1×2-inch wire is made by a different manufacturer from the one who made the $\frac{1}{2} \times 1$ wire, notch out the $\frac{1}{2}$-inch corners of the floor wire.

You now have quite a sturdy hutch from what looked like a flimsy beginning. By clipping it all together, the resulting box is extremely rigid.

Assembling hutch with J-clips and J-clip pliers.

Position of Door

Door size and position are very important, so ponder the situation. Locate the door to one side of the front because you will also need space there for a feeder and space to fill a waterer, be it a crock, bottle with tube, or valve. In addition, the door opening must be large enough to admit a nest box, which you will be putting in and taking out with some regularity.

If you use an all-wire nest box, which I will explain how to build, a door opening 12 inches wide and 11 inches high is sufficient. I recommend this size opening for both medium and small hutches. While the opening must be large enough for convenience, you are cutting into the front of the hutch and weakening it somewhat, so an opening that is unnecessarily large doesn't do it a lot of good.

I recommend a door that is 14 x 12 and swings up and in. Stand the hutch on its back, with the front up and the floor closest to you as you approach it with your wire cutters. Measure 4 inches over from the left and 4 inches from the bottom. Cut the bottom strands to the right to make a 12-inch opening. Cut up 11 inches on each side and 12 inches across the top. Do not cut these strands flush but leave stubs about ½-inch long all the way around the opening. Once you have the opening cut out, with your slip-joint pliers bend these stubs inward or outward around the outermost wire to form an opening with no sharp projections. This is important because even with flush-cutting wire cutters, the opening would be sharp if you cut the stubs off. The result would be scratched hands, arms, and rabbits.

For the door, cut 12 inches of 1 x 2 wire from the 36-inch-wide roll. Measure down 14 inches and cut, with all the cuts flush. While you are at it, measure down another 14 inches and cut another door for the next hutch and set it aside. You will have a piece 6 inches by 12 inches. Cut the stubs off that and the end of the roll. Set the small piece aside.

Latch First

Before you attach the door, attach the latch. Position it up 2 inches from the bottom of the center of the door. It fits over the strands 2 inches apart. If you lay it on a bench or the floor, you can flatten it easily over the wire with your hammer. If you wait until it's on the door to do this, you will have a most difficult time. With the latch on, fit the door **inside** the door opening and clip it with J-clips to the top of the opening.

Use a J-clip on each end and three across the middle. Do not give them a tight squeeze and the door will swing freely. Your door will overlap the sides and bottom by an inch and the latch should work easily. Give it a drop of oil if it doesn't.

Swing the door to the top of the cage, and 5 inches over from the left squeeze on the door hanger with your slip-joint pliers. When the cage is in use, the hanger will hold the door up while you reach into the cage. Give the door a push and it will swing loose and shut. The beauty of this door is that it is always inside the cage and not out in the aisle to snag your sleeve. If you forget to latch it, your rabbits cannot escape because it will stay shut no matter how hard they push it.

The hutch now looks finished, and in fact it is useable, but it needs some finishing touches. To prevent baby rabbits from falling out of the hutch if they fall out of the nest box, a "baby-saver" is needed. Take the 2-inch-wide strip you set aside when you split the 36-inch wire for front and back sections. "Stagger" it over one end on the outside at the bottom and fasten it with J-clips every 6 inches. This will close the openings at the bottom to ½ × 1 inches and will prevent the babies from falling through. Cut a two-inch strip for the front and another for the back and fasten them on. When you split another front and back section for the next hutch, clip that one on the other end. When you get to the end of the roll you will find that you will be able to build 10 hutches in this manner and have enough material for the baby-saver feature. In the meantime, save the pieces from the door openings and doors for later use as hay racks.

The Larger Rabbitry

If you plan to build a large rabbitry of more than 10 hutches, it is a good idea to buy a roll of wire for the sides of the hutches, another roll for the tops, a roll for the floors, and even another roll for the doors.

The building scheme with wire of various widths is to form the four sides from one length, bent in three 90° angles and clipped together at the fourth corner; lay on the top and then the bottom. You may want to build hutches with multiple compartments. If so, measure the length of the side wire accordingly for the entire length of the unit, and install partitions of ½ × 1-inch wire where you want them. This approach will save you some time but little money and you do sacrifice flexibility.

One other variation should be noted. If you plan to build more than 10 hutches, it is possible to buy side wire with a built-in baby-saver feature. Additional strands of wire are welded to the bottom 3 or 4 inches of the roll. If you cannot obtain baby-saver wire, you may want to buy your floor wire 36 inches wide for hutches that are 30 inches deep, and bend 3 inches up on all sides. Clip the "flaps" to the sides and you have the baby-saver.

The above plan of action for building makes for faster construction than that for less than 10 hutches. If you expect to expand to a rabbitry of more than 10 hutches, this is a wise course to take.

Hutches for Smaller Breeds

If you plan to raise Florida Whites or another small breed, you won't need hutches for does and litters as large as you do for New Zealands or other medium size rabbits although, as pointed out, you can use them.

Because I recommend 1 square foot of floor space for each pound of mature doe rabbit, a Florida White doe needs about 5 square feet. Therefore, I make hutches for Floridas the same way I do for New Zealands, except that they are a foot shorter. A hutch 2 feet wide instead of 3, but also 2½ feet deep, is in order. In fact, you can mix larger and smaller hutches in a rabbitry and keep things uniform because the depth, the distance from front to back, is the same. The height can also be the same.

To Build 10 Hutches for Smaller Breeds

Buy 100 feet of 1 x 2 wire 18 inches wide. Cut into 9-foot sections. Bend at 2 feet, 2½ feet, and 2 feet and J-clip together to form the four sides of the hutch.

Buy 21 feet of ½ x 1 wire 30 inches wide. Cut 2-foot lengths and fasten on bottom for floors. Buy 22 feet of 1 x 2 wire 30 inches wide. Cut 2-foot lengths and fasten on tops.

Buy 14 feet of 1 x 2 wire 15 inches wide. Cut off pieces 14 x 14 inches and use for doors. Cut door openings as above for medium breeds and follow instructions as given for larger cages.

It can be seen that the procedure is basically the same no matter what size cage you build. The main thing to remember is that you lose up to 2 inches each time you cut 1 x 2 wire and up to an inch each time you cut ½ x 1 wire.

Feeders

To fit out these hutches, attach a self-feeder of the hopper variety as shown in the picture. Position the trough 4 inches above the floor for small and medium breeds. The hopper portion remains outside the hutch for easy filling by the rabbit keeper. The trough is inside but off the floor. It takes up no floor space and it is high enough and narrow enough to keep the rabbits from fouling it. Hopper self-feeders are worth the money and would save cash in the long run over tin cans even if they were made of sterling silver. Farm stores and rabbitry supply houses have them in various sizes. Use wide sizes, up to 12 inches, for does and litters. Narrow sizes, 3½ to 5½ inches, are fine for single rabbits.

Hay Racks

You can make a hay rack easily with small scraps of 1 x 2 wire such as remain from door openings. Take a 6-to-8-inch square scrap and bend 2 inches of it to an angle of about 30°. Fasten the 2-inch side to the outside front of the hutch wherever it is convenient, even on the door, with a couple of J-clips. Fill the rack with a handful of hay and the rabbits will pull it through.

Watering Devices

1. A crock. If you use crocks, get the kind with a smaller inside diameter at the bottom than the top. During freezing weather, the water will expand into ice and slide up. Otherwise, it will expand out and break the crock.

2. The tube bottle waterer. The plastic bottle with the drinker tube is a big improvement over the crock. The enclosed water supply stays clean. No space is taken from the cage floor. It requires less washing than a crock. It won't work in freezing weather but ice doesn't break it either.

3. The plastic bottle with drinker valve. You make this one yourself because, surprisingly, nobody manufactures one. All it takes is a large heavy plastic bottle, such as one for bleach or soda pop, and a drinker valve designed for automatic watering systems. The bottles are free (unless they are returnable for a deposit), and the valves cost a dollar or so and are available at farm supply or rabbitry supply houses.

With a knife or drill bit make a hole in the bottle near the bottom. Coat the threads of the valve with epoxy cement and screw or push it in. Use wire to hold it onto the cage. A quart or half-gallon bottle works well and supplies plenty of water. You can use more than one per hutch if necessary. This has all the advantages and disadvantages of the tube bottle waterer and is cheaper and more durable, can supply more water, and, if large enough, can cut filling time considerably.

4. The semi-automatic watering system. This is a fine way to water a small rabbitry. You need a tank, which can be no more than a five-gallon jerry can or pail, and flexible or rigid plastic pipe leading to drinker valves at each hutch. Almost everything can be purchased locally, with the possible exception of the valves, which were developed for use with poultry. A very simple setup uses flexible black plastic pipe which can be fitted

New Zealand Whites in hutches in barn. Black tubing is for automatic watering.

A litter of young Tans in nest box.

out with various adapters, couplings, elbows, and tees. The pipe runs along the outside of the cage where it cannot be gnawed, about a foot or so above the floor. A simple hand-tapping tool makes the holes for the valves, which screw in and protrude through the cage wire. The rabbits quickly learn to drink from some of these valves by licking them. This dislodges a brass tip, letting the water spill into the rabbit's mouth. Others have a spring-activated stem, which opens when bitten and closes when released. The latter are better because they rarely leak.

Best System

5. The ultimate is the automatic watering system, which is simply the semi-automatic with a piped supply from well or city water system. It requires the above equipment and calls for a means of reducing water pressure before water enters the plastic supply pipe to the valves. A float valve in the tank (like the one in a toilet tank) is one way to reduce pressure. As the rabbits drink, the float valve allows more water to enter the tank, keeping it constantly full. Pressure reducing valves are also available. An advantage of the float valve and tank is that you can keep your system functioning in cold weather by coiling a length of heating cable inside the tank.

Nest Boxes

Place a nest box in the doe's all-wire hutch on the 27th day after you mate her. You must use one because of the open nature of the all-wire hutch.

Buy or build the all-wire next box with removable corrugated cardboard liners. This is the nest box I have used exclusively for many years and strongly recommend. It is made with ½ x 1-inch floor wire and J-clips, with metal flanges covering the top edges to protect the rabbits from injury as they hop in and out.

In very cold weather, use it with a corrugated cardboard liner, perhaps with an extra layer of corrugated cardboard or foam plastic to insulate the floor. A new liner, free of any possible germs, is used for each litter, then discarded. You can cut these corrugated liners from boxes, usually obtainable free.

In warm weather, cut cardboard for only the floor and use less bedding of shavings and straw. Leaving the wire mesh sides open improves ventilation. This guards against dampness and extreme heat, two killers. The open mesh, too, provides a fine view of the litter's daily progress.

Here's how to build yours:

For both New Zealand Whites and Florida Whites, cut out a floor section of $\frac{1}{2} \times 1$-inch 14 or 16 gauge galvanized wire that is 10×18 inches. Cut out a back section 8×10 inches and side sections 8×18 inches. For the front, cut an 8×10 piece and cut a V-shape notch as shown in the illustration. Use J-clips 4 inches apart to fasten the box together.

Cover the sharp edges along the top with flanges of galvanized metal that will also serve to clamp the corrugated liner in place. With a pair of tin snips or other metal cutters, cut the flanges from 28-gauge galvanized metal available from building and heating supply dealers. For the sides, make them 3 inches wide by 17 inches long. For the back, 3 inches by 9 inches. The front requires two flanges to fit the v-shape notch. Make them 3 inches by 5 inches each.

A simple way to shape the flanges is to bend them around a $\frac{1}{2}$-inch wooden dowel, available in hardware and building supply stores. Wear gloves to avoid cutting your fingers. Nail a piece of wood lath about $\frac{1}{4}$-inch thick and 2 or 3 inches wide, by a couple of feet long, to a work bench. If you don't have a work bench, nail the lath to a heavy plank and place that on the floor or a table.

Lay a piece of the flange-to-be on the lath, with 2 inches off and an inch on, lengthwise. Place the dowel on the sheet metal at the edge of the lath and hammer a slight curve into it by striking the dowel along its length. Then, with your thumbs on the metal, use your fingers to pull the metal around the dowel. Once you have pulled it all around, lay it on a short piece of board (a piece of 1×2 furring strip or other scrap will do) and strike it with your hammer. Turn the piece over and continue striking the board until you have the desired shape. This all takes less time than it does to tell about it. Repeat the operation for all the flanges.

Cut the cardboard liner an inch smaller all the way around than the outside dimensions of the box and score the folds with a knife. Bend it to the box shape and fit it into the box. Cut out a "second floor" of $\frac{1}{2} \times 1$ wire that is 9×17 inches and place it inside the box to prevent scratching through the cardboard.

Poke a few drainage holes through the floor. In very warm weather, cut cardboard only for the floor, instead of a liner, poking drainage holes through it. Also, because you will use no cardboard sides in hot weather, twist pieces of flexible wire around the flanges and through the side wire, to hold the flanges. This is unnecessary when using the full cardboard liner.

Tony Pisanelli builds wire hutches for sale.
Here he shows rolls of wire and finished hutches.

Tony Pisanelli shows how carrying cage opens on top.

Winter Protection

In very cold weather place additional cardboard or foam plastic on the floor, add a layer of shavings, and insert the second floor on top. The supermarket is a source of this foam plastic. Fresh meat and vegetables often come in trays of plastic foam. The shavings will absorb moisture below the second floor. Of course, use several inches of shavings and plenty of straw above the second floor, filling the nest box to the top. The doe will burrow into it to make a nest for the litter, and line it with fur from her own body.

This versatile nest box will last a lifetime. It needs no cleaning as a new liner is used each time. It works well in all kinds of weather. It is light and compatible with the all-wire hutch and can be stored on top of the hutch because of its light weight. Furthermore, if you assess your cage requirements carefully when ordering floor wire, it is possible you can build your nest boxes from floor wire remaining on a roll if you must buy it 100 or even 50 feet at a time.

A parting word about nest boxes includes two kinds never to use. The first is a plastic cat bed that some suppliers are offering as a nest box. Rabbits will eat plastic. Second, do not try to use a cardboard box alone. The doe will tip it over if she doesn't eat it first. Either way, the litter will surely be lost.

The Carrying Cage

Sooner or later you will want to transport your rabbits, either to market, to sell, or to show. The all-wire carrier or carrying cage is the best way to do so. It is light in weight and will keep the rabbits cool and well ventilated during transportation.

You can build yours from small pieces of 1 x 2 and ½ x 1 wire. After building cages and nest boxes you will find it a cinch. Dimensions of the floor should give the rabbit enough room to stretch out. Measure a stretched-out rabbit and start from there. For short hauls, the height need be no more than 8 inches. For longer trips, which would require feeding and watering along the way, you will need more height, and, in fact, a junior-size hutch.

Put your carrier together much like the nest box except with 1 x 2 wire for the sides and top and ½ x 1 for the floor. You can use ½ x 1 wire all around if you have it. Raise the floor an inch from the bottom so there is clearance underneath to provide for drainage and droppings. A metal pan underneath will catch droppings and urine. Or, you can find plastic trays or dish-pans in housewares departments of local stores and build your carriers to fit them. Put an inch or so of shavings in the tray and attach to the carrier with short hooks of wire or small springs.

Cut the top an inch or two larger than the floor and bend corners to fit over the sides. Hinge it from the back with J-clips. This is a substitute for the door cut in the hutch. A dog leash snap fastener is one way to clip it closed.

After building a few wire hutches, nest boxes, and carrying cages, you will find the work goes quickly and enjoyably. The techniques for all this wire working are the same. You really can't make an error if you measure carefully, because the wire is in effect a grid that assures all your equipment will come out square and true. It won't be long, before you will be considering building hutches for others, to make additional cash for yourself, as I will describe in Chapter 9.

Chapter 6

The Third Key to Success:
The Right Feed

If the first two keys to success are the right rabbit and the right housing, then the third, which unlocks the door to your objective, is the right feed.

Nothing could be simpler than feeding rabbits successfully, yet many raisers complicate their lives unnecessarily by trying to find alternatives to what the rabbit really needs. The rabbit pellet is a mixture of everything the rabbit needs for nutrition. It is a combination of grains and forage plus vitamins and minerals, all tucked into a bite-size pellet a little smaller than a pencil eraser. Every time the rabbit eats one he gets the complete nutritional mixture of protein, fat, and fiber. If only you could feed your children this way!

It's true rabbits will eat and can be fed carrots, lettuce, other greens, and other root crops, and often it is advisable to give these feeds. But each of them contains only **some** of what a rabbit needs for growth and health. The rabbit pellet contains **all** of what the animal requires.

Buy your rabbit pellets in 50- or 100-pound bags. You will find that 100 pounds will store nicely in a metal garbage can, which, with its lid, will protect them from moisture and prevent an invasion of mice. There is no reason to have any mice on the scene if you use the hopper feeder, provide the correct amount of feed, and store pellets in a metal garbage can. Mice will arrive

Rabbit pellets keep well in a covered metal garbage can.

unannounced, undoubtedly, if you spill feed, leave too much in the hoppers, or leave the bag unprotected.

Almost all brands of rabbit pellets will do the job, despite advertising that claims one company's product is better than another's. Sure, there probably is one best brand, but the differences among most are so slight as to be negligible. If you have a local or regional feed company, the pellets may be fresher than those of a national brand manufactured miles away, and you may be able to get them cheaper because transportation is a big part of the cost.

Check the size of the pellet. If it is too long—more than ¼ inch—the rabbits will bite off only part of it and let the rest drop through the wire mesh floor to the manure below.

Specifications

Protein levels in the 16–18 percent range are sufficient for does and litters, as well as bucks and growing juniors. Higher protein levels are not necessary, but if you plan to supplement the pellets liberally with other feeds, and you can find higher protein pellets, they are worth getting. Some manufacturers list 20–21 percent protein. Feed these with hay and other feeds that we will mention in a moment. Look for a high fiber content—in the 15–16 percent range. High fiber content is very important to permit good digestion and to avoid intestinal troubles. Fat is a major ingredient. It should be about 3 percent. Only one type of pellet is needed for does, litters, bucks and juniors.

Pellets should be hard and relatively dust-free. Old and worn pelleting machines often will produce a pellet with rough edges. These rub against each other when bagged to produce dust which rabbits won't eat. Dust weighs. You pay for it. Rabbits shun it.

Use a hopper feeder for pellets. You load it from outside the hutch. It takes no space on the hutch floor and it keeps the feed clean. If you feed from outside the hutch (and you will water the rabbits without having to open the hutch door), feeding and watering will take you as little as a mere minute a day.

Before I leave the discussion of pellets for the time being—we'll cover how much and when to feed in the next chapter—let me say you certainly should expect to purchase them in a feed and grain store, or in some cases a hardware store or supermarket. Avoid the pet store. Prices are much higher there because the pellets are put up in small packages.

You don't have to buy all your feed. If you make pellets the primary, basic feed, you can provide supplemental feeds that will cost you little or nothing and add to the variety of the rabbits' diet.

Other Feeds

Let's start with feeds available right in your kitchen. Here are some you may have from time to time:

- **Leftover breakfast cereal, perhaps with milk.**
- **Dry bread or toast.**
- **Stale crackers.**
- **Outside leaves of lettuce.**
- **Celery tops.**
- **Carrot tops and peelings.**
- **Potato peelings.**
- **Apple peelings and cores (especially if you make pies or applesauce and have a lot).**
- **Beet and turnip tops and peelings.**

All the greens and roots should be washed and fresh. Conspicuously absent from the list are cabbage, cauliflower, and Brussels sprouts, which can cause stomach trouble. Avoid all these.

Now let's take a look around the average small yard for rabbit food:

- **Dried grass clippings (but not if the lawn has been sprayed with chemicals).**
- **Dandelions dug from the lawn.**
- **Plantain dug from the lawn.**

Do not feed any leaves raked up, especially rhododendron leaves, which are poisonous.

If you have a section of lawn, in the backyard perhaps, that you can let grow tall, you can cut it, dry the grass in the sun, and feed it as hay. You can usually get two or three cuttings per season. In fact, you might plant some of your land in alfalfa or red clover. Oats could be planted, cut, dried in the sun, and fed without threshing.

Useful Plants

Let's venture afield a bit before we go back to our own vegetable garden. Here are some useful plants you might find:

Blackberry or raspberry—the leaves can be fed if the rabbits have a touch of diarrhea. It's not a bad idea to keep some handy in season if you can find them.

Wild carrot or Queen Anne's lace—here's a plant you might find in a pasture, and it's a fine green food.

Hogweed or cow parsnip—found along the highway on a sandy embankment or just out in a field.

Clover—especially the red-blossomed type. Feed small amounts green, or cut and dry it and feed it as hay.

Field corn gleaned after the harvest—if you ask a farmer, he will probably let you take a feed sack into his corn field after he has harvested his crop with heavy machinery. You will find ears the harvester missed and if you don't take them, the crows will. I like to toss them into an empty rabbit cage as a miniature corn crib and let them dry, then toss them one at a time into a cage and let the occupant enjoy corn on the cob.

Vegetables

Now let's go back to our own yard and the vegetable garden. Rabbit manure does much for the development of the garden. It seems only fair to let the rabbits have something back and it is great to have rabbits around to use up the vegetables that you don't. There's never any waste in the garden with rabbits backing up the family appetite. When I plant my garden I usually plant more than I want because sometimes I get less than I want, depending on the weather and my ability as a gardener. Nevertheless, I always plant more than the family can use of certain vegetables, such as:

Carrots. I grow wide rows of carrots on raised beds to get long roots in my heavy soil. I like to grow Danvers half-longs and pull them small for the family. But they don't always get used small and when they get big they go to the rabbits. Chantenay is a large, stout carrot that I grow especially for the rabbits. You can pull them small for your own table or let them get big and almost woody for the rabbits.

In fact, you can pile leaves or hay on them in the fall after you have harvested all you can use. During the winter you can dig through the snow and the hay and pull some of the sweetest carrots you ever ate right through February in Vermont, which has one of the coldest climes in the country. You may not even want to share them with the rabbits, but you should, especially when their water tends to freeze regularly. That's when they really enjoy the succulent roots.

Another way to preserve them for winter is to pack them in sand or sawdust in a cool cellar, or barrel or can sunk in the ground. My barn has a gravel floor and I have sunk a garbage can into the floor in one corner. I throw in carrots and sand and fill it up. Then I put a couple of hay bales on top. All winter I can pull carrots out of there any time I (or the rabbits) want them. This system works well for other roots, too, such as:

Rutabagas. You may call them yellow turnips or Swede turnips. These are just as good as carrots for a winter feed. Pack them in sand or mulch them under hay, straw, or leaves, as above.

Beets are also good rabbit food. Regular garden beets are fine. Mangel or sugar beets are even better—and bigger. They are best when left stored until about January. Mangel or sugar beet seeds can be found in some seed catalogs and also in farm supply stores. In Europe they are used for cattle feed and are sometimes called stock beets. You can feed the tops as you trim the roots in the fall, and save the roots for winter.

Jerusalem artichokes aren't really roots, but tubers. Some people like them and some don't. If your family doesn't, plant them anyway and feed them to the rabbits.

A parsnip is a root. It looks like a white carrot. It tastes best when left all winter, mulched, and dug in the spring. It is also appreciated the most then, because that's a season when you aren't likely to have many other roots around yet, as you have barely planted your seeds.

Comfrey is a plant I grow expressly for rabbits. You can feed them the green leaves or dry them and feed during the fall or winter like hay. The same goes for lettuce, kale, chicory, endive, and celery leaves.

Sunflowers produce wonderful seeds that will put a great coat of fur on your rabbits, because they contain oil. I plant sunflowers on the north side of the garden along a fence, behind some flowers, and wherever else I can find space. They don't need much ground, but they grow about 6 to 8 feet high and tower over everything, until their massive seed-blossom heads bend and sway in the autumn wind. As the seeds mature, cut the heads and hang them in the garage, barn, porch, attic, or wherever you can to let them dry, but safe from the birds that love them so. To feed them, break the heads into pieces and toss them into the cage. The rabbits will pick the seeds, spit out the shells, and get fat and furry on the nutmeats, which are very high in protein.

Timely Crops

What's really great about the garden feeds for rabbits is that they ordinarily flourish at about the same time your biggest crop of rabbits is hungry. While rabbits breed all year long, there's no question that spring is the time of year when you will be producing more and bigger litters. It's the natural time of the year for rabbit production. As the litters grow, so grows the garden and you will find that summer and autumn are times of the year when you have the most hungry rabbits and the most garden food to satisfy that hunger. Gardens and rabbits work so well together, it's a shame to have one without the other. Even the smallest piece of residential property can produce a tremendous amount of supplementary feed for a trio of rabbits and their offspring.

Additional feeds abound elsewhere. Stale bakery products that might be thrown away often can be obtained. Dry bread and rolls are especially valuable. Visit a commercial bakery and find out what happens to leftover goods. You might be able to buy them cheap or get them free. You won't know unless you investigate.

Your supermarket produce man may be willing to let you have a crate of trimmings from his vegetables. Carrot and beet tops, often with misshapen or small roots included, along with lettuce leaves and celery tops, can be found in these crates (and the crates, the wirebound wooden ones, are wonderful for transporting and even shipping rabbits). Wash these greens carefully.

In some places you may be able to obtain spilled whole grains, such as at a railroad siding near a bread bakery. A friend of mine has gathered many sacks of whole and cracked wheat at such locations over the past several years.

Ingenuity, initiative, and effort, without worrying about what your friends will think when they see you scavenging, will pay off. Some raisers love the challenge of seeing how much of their feed they can get for nothing. I recall a friend of mine in New Jersey, a big executive in a three-piece suit, who filled a paper bag with plantain, clover, and dandelions while he waited for his morning bus to Manhattan. He nonchalantly stuffed the bag into his briefcase each spring and summer morning, then carried the greens to work and home again that night to the rabbits. He didn't worry about what anybody thought of it. Neither did the rabbits.

Cost of Meat

All such activity will help cut the costs of putting meat on your table. And we will cover ways to obtain cash income from your rabbit project than can bring these costs to zero **and below.** It's true, with some effort you will be putting rabbits on your table for little or nothing—or at a profit in your pocket.

Let's take a look at what your costs per pound will be, depending upon how much you pay for feed and how much you have to buy.

Your New Zealands or Florida Whites should produce a pound of live weight gain on no more than 4 pounds of pellets or the equivalent. Let's forget for a moment that your New Zealands will eat more per day for fewer days and that the dressout percentage of the Florida White doubtless will be greater. The fact is you will be putting about the same amount of feed into either animal to get a pound of live weight. It's true you probably can get more meat on less feed with the Floridas, but not significantly more in a small operation.

Feed Costs

If the feed cost is $11 per 100 pounds, which is a 1983 figure, the feed cost is of course 11 cents a pound. If you feed 4 pounds per pound of gain, that's 44 cents a pound, which, by the way, includes feed for the buck and of course the doe. For the first couple of weeks or so of the litter's life, they will be living on the doe's milk. The doe will require plenty of feed to produce that milk. In the last six weeks until slaughter, the litter will eat both pellets (and other feed) and milk.

If you figure a 50 percent dressout, at 11 cents a pound of feed or 44 cents per live weight pound of gain, the meat on your table will cost you 88 cents a pound maximum, based on feed costs only.

If you begin to figure the cost of the breeding rabbits, cages, feeders, and other equipment, you will perhaps question the wisdom of the entire project, but before you get discouraged, let's look at the big picture and all the ways to cut your costs. For the moment, let's consider feed costs only.

Supplemental Feeds

In the paragraph above, I mentioned various feeds you can get at little or no cost. Depending upon how resourceful you are, you easily can cut your costs in half by supplementing the pellets with these various feeds. By cutting costs in half, your cost of meat drops to 44 cents a pound dressed, considering feed costs alone.

Sale of Pelts

A dried white rabbit pelt from a fryer-size (4 pounds) rabbit is worth 50 cents or more. Save these until you obtain a quantity the purchaser will buy and which can be shipped economically. If you learn to tan the pelt, your income can easily double. (Some rabbit raisers become fascinated with fur and learn to sew hats, mittens, muffs, collars, and coats—even making stuffed toys for sale.) To stay on the conservative side, let's figure 50 cents. If you save 50 cents on a 4-pound rabbit, you save 12½ cents per pound, reducing your costs. Now you are down to 31½ cents per pound. Let's call it 32 cents.

Sale of Meat Rabbits

Now we are ready to make the operation really pay. Let's say you want to eat only **some** of the rabbits you produce. You wish to sell some to others.

There are brokers and processors who will pay from 60 cents to $1 or more per pound live weight. Some will pick up your rabbits. Others want you to deliver. To calculate this easily and conservatively, we'll call this 60 cents a pound.

We have seen that your two does can produce 64 rabbits per year or 128 pounds dressed. Maybe you don't want to eat that much. It would mean rabbit on the table every 6 days. Suppose you are willing to part with two rabbits from each litter, or 16 per year. You've still got rabbit on the table every 8 days.

At 60 cents a pound, each rabbit will bring you $2.40 as a 4-pounder. It cost you $1.76 to feed it if you fed all pellets. That's 44 cents a pound. Your margin over feed costs is 16 cents a pound or 64 cents. If you cut your feed costs in half by supplementing the pellets your cost is 22 cents a pound or 88 cents a rabbit, and your margin is now $1.52 per rabbit. Again, let's be conservative and call it 64 cents per rabbit or $1.28 for the two of them. If the two were sold out of a litter of eight, leaving you six for the freezer and table, you cut the cost of the remaining six by about 21 cents each or a nickel a pound.

Subtract that nickel from the 32 cents you are now putting into the pound of dressed, edible meat, and the cost is down to 27 cents a pound. It's beginning to look pretty good. You could sell even more of them for meat and make it look better. (Some people have been known to sell them **all**, take the money, and buy steak!)

Sale of Live Rabbits

There is no question about it—sooner or later you are going to run into people who want to do what you are doing. They will want to raise meat for their own tables and will need some breeding stock. You will find people who want to buy some of your young rabbits to raise themselves. When you do, you will be able to forego the sale of meat rabbits or sell additional rabbits, depending on how many you want to keep. Doubtless the first year you will be able to more than recover the cost of your initial breeding stock—although the expense should not be figured as a one-year deal, but amortized over the breeding life of the rabbit. For does, that's about 3 years. For bucks, about 5. Right now let's not build that into your feed costs, but if each year you sold enough breeding stock to pay your initial costs, the fact is you would gain three times what you paid for them (not even counting future inflation that would increase your gain). That will reduce your costs even more—in fact, you are closing in on a no-cost situation. Meat on your table for less than pennies a pound. Meat on your table for nothing at all but your own labor, if you can call this work.

Here are more ways to make money, and some of them do constitute work. I found it enjoyable, and you may too, as many have.

Sale of Rabbit Hutches

If you built your own hutches, people who buy breeding stock from you will admire them. Certainly they will need hutches of their own. You can build them for sale, and your selling price should be about twice the cost of materials. Once again, it is not reasonable, from a business standpoint, to recover the cost of your hutches the first year. I have some that are 20 years old, but amortization over half that time or less is reasonable. Wire costs keep rising and the hutches I built years ago are worth much more than what they cost. Some of my oldest hutches cost less than $5 to build and are worth $25 or more now, even after all these years. It took me over an hour to build the first one, but now I can build a hutch in less than 30 minutes, all with hand tools. I like doing it, too. It's quiet and relaxing and easy and just about impossible to do incorrectly. Any amateur's first attempt can look as professional as a hutch from a leading manufacturer.

Sale of Materials

Let's suppose you don't want to build the hutches, and your breeding stock customers want to build their own. You can purchase the wire in 100-foot rolls and cut off sections required for individual hutches, marking up the cut wire price enough to cover the costs of your own hutches initially, and eventually, to provide yourself with a source of income that can easily cover the costs of your hutches and feed. Much more can come of it. For years my sons and I built hutches for sale to pet stores. We put them on consignment, which was a good arrangement for the boys and me as well as the store. If the store didn't sell a hutch as fast as I needed one to sell myself, it was still mine and I could take it back, promising the storekeeper another soon. This can provide a nice source of extra money—and I'll expand on how to get it in another chapter.

Sale of Manure

The end of the income story? Not really. There's more money to be made.

As a gardener, I like to use the rabbit droppings on vegetables, flowers, and shrubs. You may, too. I have found, however, that rabbit manure is in demand by serious rose gardeners. This revelation has led me to expect cash income from rabbit manure rather than simply saving me the cash I might spend on fertilizer.

For a number of years I sacked it up in the 50-pound bags the pellets came in. It doesn't weigh 50 pounds, and it isn't sold by weight, either, but rather by volume. Some bags weigh more than others, depending upon moisture content, primarily. I put the bags on consignment at a local garden center. Each bag brought me about $5, the cost of a bag of feed at the time. Certainly you don't get a bag of manure for every bag of feed, although that would be terrific! But for every bag you sell, that's a free bag of feed.

Sale of Compost

I used to shred up leaves from the trees in my yard and mix them with the manure, about 50–50, making fantastic compost. Some hay and straw that fell through the cage floor were also part of the mixture. I let it sit for several months in a pile until it decomposed and was black and crumbly. Into the bag and down to the garden center it went.

Use of Manure

I rationalize my use of the manure now as a way of not buying fertilizer for lawn and garden. It's true I still buy some garden fertilizer. But for the lawn, I spread the dry rabbit manure and forget about the expensive fertilizers. I get some weeds out of it, but I always seemed to anyway when I used the more expensive

Florida White.

Florida White.

products. I'm not as fussy about weeds as I used to be, and I can always take care of them with a liquid weed killer in a hose sprayer.

Swapping Meats

All of these efforts certainly can reduce your costs to nothing. Rabbit meat can go on your table for pennies or nothing or even make you a profit. And it doesn't even all have to be rabbit meat. Some butchers or freezer lockers will swap you other meat for your rabbit. You might offer the butcher two pounds of rabbit meat for a pound of steak or ham or whatever you want. Many rabbit raisers do just that. I know one who raises rabbits in his garage but doesn't eat them—he trades for prime ribs. It's just like being a rancher in the Wild West, except that it all takes place at the end of a garage.

Savings on Taxes

There's still another way that rabbits can cost you less. Whenever you buy yourself a steak (or just a can of beans), you have to pay cash. That cash most likely comes out of a paycheck. As you very well know, your paycheck is reduced substantially by income taxes. Depending upon your tax bracket, you have to earn substantially more than a dollar to take a dollar home. When you get a dollar home, if you could save it instead of spending it, you have a chance to earn something on it. So for every dollar's worth of meat you raise, you save yourself more, because you would have had to earn more than a dollar to get it. It's another way of looking at the big picture. And it's another way of either saving or increasing your disposable income—increasing your real net worth.

We began this chapter on feeding by figuring our costs. It's nice to be able to wind it up by discussing our profits.

Chapter 7

Putting It All Together

Your rabbits are home, in their hutches, and the feed is at hand. The three keys to success are yours, so here's where you take charge.

Each rabbit has its own hutch. If you have them in tiers, put the buck on the bottom and the does on top. It will be easier to mate them when it's time, and it will keep the buck cooler, which is important.

If you have three young rabbits to raise, you will want to make sure, first of all, that they have a constant supply of fresh water. That means at least once every day you should give fresh water. Dump out what's left of yesterday's water and rinse out the crock. That's not necessary if you are using a water bottle. Once a week wash out the crocks or bottles with detergent, making certain you rinse them well. No rabbit wants to drink soapy water.

Now for the feed. It's a good idea, when you first bring them to their new home, to continue them with the same brand of pellets they have been eating. If you want to switch later, that's fine, but for now give them what they've been used to. It will make them feel at home right away, and get them off to a good start at your place.

How Much to Feed

Young, growing rabbits should be given all the pellets they can eat. No more, however. If you use a hopper feeder, put in about 4 or 5 ounces in the morning for New Zealands, about 3 ounces for the Floridas. Check the hopper in the evening. If it's empty, put in more than you put in that morning. If there are pellets remaining, put in less. Check the hopper the first thing in the morning and repeat the process, checking it again the same evening. Learn how much they will eat, and provide that amount. Give a little too much at first, which you will probably do anyway. But you don't want stale pellets hanging around in the feeder. For one thing, they lose palatability. For another, they will attract mice.

Your young rabbits should have a big appetite if they are just-weaned youngsters. They will maintain this appetite until they are 6 to 8 months of age for New Zealands, a month or so less for Floridas. You want them to eat all they want to make sure they gain the proper amount of weight.

Leave Them Alone

When you get the rabbits home, leave them alone for a couple of days as much as possible. Family members, especially children, will be fascinated by the new arrivals, and will want to pet them, hold them, and give them a lot of attention. Give the rabbits a break. They are new around here. They are uncertain of their surroundings. They are young and they are not sure whether they like you or what's going to happen next. So give them a couple of days to become acclimated to their new home. Be certain to keep dogs and cats away at this time, and **all the time**.

Don't give the young rabbits any greens, but feed them all the dry hay they can eat. You may also provide dry bread, oats, and leftover breakfast cereal, but no greenstuff when they are young, or it may give diarrhea.

You may give small amounts—a piece of carrot, a leaf or two of lettuce—to rabbits after they have reached about 4 months of age. Then, as they get older, you may **gradually** increase amounts so long as you make pellets, or a combination of pellets and grains that will deliver the nutrient levels the pellets will, the mainstay of their diets. Your rabbits are growing and need all the nutrition they can get. When they reach the adult stage, their diet can include more supplemental feed.

Adult rabbits should receive all the feed they will consume in about an hour. Adult Florida Whites will eat about 3 ounces of pellets or the equivalent. Adult New Zealands require about 5 or 6 ounces.

Check Daily

Each day run your hand over each animal's shoulders, loin, and rump. Feed to keep the animal solid but not fat and certainly not flabby on either the thin or heavy side. You want to build and maintain good flesh tone—muscle. Each rabbit is a bit different. Some eat more than others. Some eat faster.

When you feed your rabbits, there should be no feed left over from the previous day. The rabbits should not, however, greet you at feeding time by trying to tear the door off the hutch to get at the feed scoop. Don't be a slave to instructions in this or any other book. Feed for a good solid but trim rabbit, whatever that takes. What I've said already regarding amounts is just a guide. It's also true that some rabbits, if given a piece of carrot, will let it stay in the hutch uneaten for more than an hour—perhaps all day. That's okay. On the other hand, believe it or not, some rabbits won't even touch a carrot. If one remains untasted for a couple of days, give it to another rabbit, and try feeding the first one something else.

You may feed your rabbits twice a day or even more often if you like so long as the total amount of feed doesn't change. I feed once a day, in the evening. What is important is to establish a routine, a feeding pattern. Some rabbit raisers feed both morning and night, as I suggested earlier. If you feed supplemental feeds, you might want to give pellets at night and the other feed in the morning.

All green feeds should be washed and dry. Not that lettuce leaves should be dehydrated, but they shouldn't be dripping wet or left in a wet heap to ferment and mold. And they shouldn't be left on the floor of the hutch for a long period. I think it's perfectly okay to feed greens on the floor of an all-wire hutch if it is in small amounts and eaten right away so it doesn't get soiled. If you put them in a hay rack they usually wind up on the floor anyway. It's the handiest place for many items, such as apples, carrots, and the like.

Time to Mate

When Florida Whites reach about 5 months of age and New Zealands about 6 or 7, it's time to mate them. With the Floridas, which mature rapidly, I say 5 months or 5 pounds, whichever comes first, for the does. Bucks aren't ready until they are 5 or even 6 months old. New Zealand does should weigh 9 pounds and the bucks at least 8 before mating. The bucks usually aren't ready until 6 or 8 months. Some people mate the does at 5 months, although most don't. A lot depends upon how fast the rabbits are maturing—some simply grow a lot faster than others.

It's a good idea to get the does mated right on time and not to let them get too old or too heavy before they have the first litter. Let's suppose your doe is 6 months old but you don't think you want a litter just yet for some reason. It's a good idea to mate her anyway. If you let the doe get older and heavier she may develop fat that can choke off the fallopian tubes and prevent the eggs from descending to be fertilized at mating time.

Mating Time Is Any Time

When is mating time? Just about any time after your rabbits become sexually mature, at the ages outlined above. Female rabbits have no cycle. Or, maybe they do. Scientists don't agree on this. It's possible there's a day or two per month when they won't conceive, although this is debatable. It is also inconsequential because you don't know when it is anyway. So mate your rabbits when **you** want them mated.

To do so, take the doe to the buck (never the other way around), put her in his hutch, and wait a very short time, ordinarily. Rabbits mate readily, and are famous or notorious for this behavior. The buck will fall over backwards or on his side after mating is complete.

Sometimes you may think the doe does not want to accept the buck. She may even put up a bit of a fight—running away, growling, hitting him with her paws. This usually is simply part of the mating routine. She's playing hard to get. Watch her tail. If it twitches, she really wants to mate sooner or later.

On the other hand, there are times when the doe will not cooperate (hardly ever are there times when the buck is not interested). That being the case, take her out and try again after a few hours or the next day. If she still won't cooperate after some time, leave her in the buck's hutch and put him in hers. Let them stay in each other's hutches overnight. The next day put the doe back in her own hutch where the buck is temporarily residing. Having acquired the scent of the buck overnight in his hutch, it's a good bet she will be interested now.

Still, however, there may be times when this method will not work. If so, hold her by the scruff of the neck with your right hand, and place the left one under her belly. Place her in the buck's cage in this position and restrain her for mating. The buck will mount her despite the presence of your hands.

We mentioned the descent of the eggs for fertilization. It is the stimulation by mating that signals the eggs to descend. This descent requires about 8 hours. Therefore, many successful rabbit breeders take the doe back to the buck for a second mating about 8 hours after the first one. This is good insurance, in case the first mating didn't "take" because the sperm was not viable when the eggs descended.

That's about all there is to mating rabbits.

But Is She Pregnant?

A rabbit really isn't pregnant until you **know** she is. How do you know?

First, you can test mate her to find out. To do that, about a week after mating, a date you duly marked on a hutch record card affixed to the doe's hopper feeder or elsewhere on the hutch, you put her back in with the buck. If she whines, growls, flattens out on the hutch floor, or runs away from the buck as if she really means to avoid him, it's a good bet she is pregnant, although not a certainty.

About two weeks after mating, you can palpate the doe, or feel for the babies. Place her on a flat surface and hold the scruff of the neck with your left hand, if you are right-handed. (You lefties will have to figure out what to do by yourselves.) With your right hand, feel the **sides** of her belly carefully, gently. You should feel some marble-sized objects, which are the developing young. They will be on each **side** of the belly, not right down the middle opposite the spine. (Any marble-sized objects you feel in that location will be manure.)

If you don't feel any developing babies, put her back in with the buck. You will have lost only two weeks instead of the month that gestation requires.

Baby rabbits in nest of straw and mother's fur.

If you do feel those, you can bet she's pregnant, and that the babies will be born about 31 days after mating. On the 28th day, give her a nest box with shavings and straw; a lot of it in cold weather and a modest amount during warmer times.

Meanwhile, keep feeding the doe her normal amount of feed. Do not increase her feed until after the youngsters are born. There are a couple of reasons for this. First, she may not be pregnant after all, and you don't want to get her overly fat if that is the case. Second, even if she is, added weight can cause her difficulty when giving birth.

You will note that a day or two before the young are born she may just about quit eating pellets. That's a good time to give her some greens. After the litter is born, the greens are again especially appreciated. You will also want to increase the amount of pellets or other dry feed you give her to all she will consume, making certain, of course, that no feed is left over from day to day to become stale, moldy, or attract unwanted diners such as mice.

When the Litter is Born

Expect your litter on the 31st day after mating. Some are born a day or so earlier and some arrive later. Usually a larger litter is born early and a small litter arrives a day or two later. The doe will pull fur and line the nest box with it. You will have provided a couple of inches of shavings plus a quantity of straw in the box. She will arrange all that to her liking and after she lines it with fur, deliver the litter and cover them with more fur from her belly and chest. It is time for you to do absolutely nothing. In the first place, she needs no help. In the second, peace and quiet will do the most to assure a safe, live delivery. You should stay away. Keep kids, dogs, cats, neighbors, and everybody else away for 3 or 4 days. The day **after** the litter is born, however, you, the rabbit keeper, may remove the nest box for an inspection. First, approach the hutch quietly. Second, put in some tempting green feed to distract the doe. Third, carefully remove the nest box to a location out of sight of the doe. You will see a pile of fur in there, quivering slightly. With a short, blunt stick, not your hands, carefully push some of the fur aside. The idea is to keep your hands, with their scent, out of things. You should be able to count the babies and mark the quantity on the hutch card. If there are any dead ones, remove and bury them. Then, with the stick, push the fur back the way it was and return the box to its original position.

Your nest box has no cover on it if you use the type I recommend. That means you can see into it every day as you feed the doe. Keep an eye on it to make sure no youngsters fall out or become separated from the rest of the litter. If they do, pick 'em up and put 'em back in, that's all.

If you have bred two does at the same time, which is a fine idea, after a couple of days or so you may want to even up the litter size. If one of your rabbits has nine or ten and the other has only six or eight, transfer some of the larger litter to the other doe. Simply put them in at the bottom of the heap. Remember, a doe has only eight places at the table. If there are more than eight youngsters, somebody occasionally goes without. Doe rabbits have been known to raise huge litters (would you believe 15?) but your does will do better if they have no more than eight. Here's another chance for me to put in a plug for the smaller breeds, such as the Floridas. They don't usually have more than eight.

Provide A Lot of Food

For the next 8 weeks provide your doe and her litter all the feed they can consume. Keep the green stuff away from the youngsters. It will give them diarrhea and could kill them. I like to make sure that my litters have plenty of good dry hay. It seems to be an aid to digestion as they make the transition from mother's milk to solid food. Crimped or rolled oats are especially good for the transition, too. We've got delicate stomachs to consider. So be careful with them. Dry bread, milk, cereal—these are all fine and welcome now.

Before your rabbits are 3 weeks old they will be bounding out of the nest box. Up until that time greens are fine for the mother. After that, eliminate them because the offspring will eat them. Keep the dry, solid food, with pellets as the mainstay, in front of them at all times.

Remove Nest Box

In warm weather, you can take out the nest box when the litter is 3 weeks old. I like to keep it in longer when the weather is cold. Depending upon the weather and the protection you have from it for your hutch, you may want to leave it in longer, but if you have a well-sheltered hutch you can take it out at 4 weeks in almost any kind of weather. When I take it out, I like to put in a board about 8 x 12 inches and place the shavings and straw from the box on top of it. The litter will huddle and sleep there for a few days before knocking it all apart, but the transition seems to be a good one. I like to avoid abrupt changes of all kinds. Keep it smooth is my motto; bridge each change in life-style for the young rabbits.

Beginning at age 4 weeks for the litter, I like to attempt to mate the doe for the next litter. Because I like my litters born at midweek when my children and the neighborhood's are in school and things are nice and quiet, I mate my does on week-ends. I have more time then, what with a job to go to Monday through Friday. It means that weekends are the time to put in the nest boxes, too, and I like the routine. You could arrange it for Wednesdays or any other day, but the idea is to **have a routine**. That way you are less likely to forget to mate the does and put in the boxes. In any case, once a week after the litter is 4 weeks old, you should mate the does until palpation convinces you the does are expecting.

Remating

It's especially important to get your does remated while they are still nursing. That's because they are slim and trim at this time. If you rest them after a litter is weaned, they are likely to put on internal fat that will prevent conception. Keep them pregnant as often as possible. Remember, production is what you are after. Ignore the temptation to give them a rest. You don't want to encourage internal fat to develop as eggs won't de-scend and be fertilized, and rabbits won't be born. Running with the litter, they stay slim and will conceive. So try to get them mated before you wean the litter.

Depending upon how successful you are at remating the doe, you will plan weaning accordingly. If the doe is mated back at 4 weeks, plan to wean the litter at 7, giving the doe a week without them to prepare for the next bunch. If at 5 weeks, wean them at 8. Some breeders mate them back sooner—say 3 weeks —so weaning time comes at 6 weeks. Such a routine would pro-duce about six litters per year. R. M. Lockley, the British natural-ist, in his excellent book **The Private Life of the Rabbit**, points out that **wild** rabbits have several litters, with post-partum re-mating, in the spring, and few if any litters in the fall and early winter. I like to take advantage of the natural breeding time of spring and remate my does when litters are about 4 weeks old in the spring—if a small litter is being nursed, even sooner. Right now (in March), for example, I've got a doe with a litter of only four. She had seven but three froze because she didn't make the greatest nest I've ever seen. I'm mating her back at 3 weeks of litter age and hoping for another litter in early May. The four she has are not a strain on her. If she had eight, I'd give them all some more time. In fact, if I had another small litter of four, I'd take them all away, give them to the other doe, and remate her post-partum like Lockley's British wild ones.

Weaning

Weaning is not difficult. It simply means taking them away from the mother. You can wean rabbits at 4 to 8 weeks. Or you can leave them with her until they are 12 weeks, sometimes even longer, especially if you leave the young does. I've left young does with the dam, in the fall and over the winter, until the youngsters were ready to mate. You can't leave young bucks with the dam and other does. They'll impregnate the does and fight with each other. Give each buck a separate hutch.

A good weaning routine is to remove the largest of the youngsters first, and then remove the rest of the litter, at intervals of a day or two, one at a time. This seems easier on both doe and litter, and by leaving the smaller ones until last every one of them seems to cope with the process satisfactorily. You may put all the does in one hutch and all the bucks in another. Or you may slaughter and dress them and pop them into the freezer one at a time, depending upon your use for them.

Another good weaning approach is to remove the doe and let the young stay in the hutch in which they were born. They will get along for several more weeks this way, with no fighting, in most cases. They will also continue to gain well in their familiar surroundings.

If you are raising both young fryer meat rabbits and older roasters or stewers, a good procedure is to utilize the bucks as the fryers. By butchering them early you avoid the problems of fighting. The young does will usually get along nicely for weeks and even months, especially if left in their own hutch.

There is no hard and fast rule, and you should develop your own procedures, and stay flexible, too. Sometimes you may want to wean them all at the same time. Sometimes you may not.

Chapter 8

Meat on the Table

Slaughtering rabbits is not my idea of a good time. I do not enjoy getting them ready for the table. It has to be done, however, and I'm the one around here who has to do it. A long time ago I resolved to get it done quickly, easily, and well, and I'm going to tell you how it's done.

A moment of digression seems in order. Meat does not originate in the back room of the supermarket in plastic wrap. It gets there from the farm via the slaughterhouse and packing plant.

Young rabbits are attractive. Some say cute or even adorable. So are young lambs, calves, chickens, ducks, and, it seems to me, pigs. Before you can eat them, somebody has to kill them. Here's how to do it.

No Audience

First, find a time when you will have no audience. Slaughtering rabbits is a little like hanging wallpaper. You don't need anybody around to get in the way or make you nervous. It is a very exacting job and you have to do it right the first time. I like to choose a Saturday morning when the family is out shopping or otherwise occupied away from home.

Second, select an appropriate location away from the passing parade. Don't do it in the middle of the backyard where the neighbors can watch. I use the garage, or, in extremely cold weather, the basement.

Mount a pair of meat hooks on a board measuring about 6 by 12 inches, and hang it from a wall or the ceiling on a sturdy wire at shoulder height. Puncture the top of a plastic garbage or leaf bag and place it over the board, with the hooks protruding. If the bag does not hang open, tear it part way down the front. What you are going to do is hang the rabbit by the hind feet with its head down into the bag.

Have a table available with a covered pot of ice cold water (put cubes in if you have to) large enough to hold the rabbit. Unless you plan to move to the kitchen to cut up the carcass, you will also need to have a butcher block cutting board and a boning knife.

Two Tools

You need just two other tools. A length of hardwood, about 1 inch in diameter and 16 inches long, is used to stun the animal. I use an oak dowel of these dimensions. A skinning knife can be just about any small, very sharp pointed instrument. I like to use a round-bladed modelmaker's X-Acto knife or a single-edge razor blade.

With everything in readiness, I put the rabbit in a box or other carrier, and then I weigh it and record the live weight. I then hold it by the scruff of the neck in my left hand and strike it sharply behind the ears at the base of the skull with the dowel in my right. A single, well-aimed blow delivered with considerable force is the intention. If carried out, the rabbit will never know what hit him. If you find it easier, you may hold the rabbit by the loin, just forward of the hind legs.

Hang the rabbit on the hooks by inserting them between the tendons and bones of each hind leg. With its head hanging down into the plastic bag, sever the head and let it fall into the bag. The rabbit will now bleed and the blood will drain into the bag. It's important to cut off the head immediately to avoid a blood clot in the neck area, which can discolor the meat.

With your skinning knife or other sharp blade, carefully cut the skin around the hind legs just above the hock. Do not cut the tendon that is holding the rabbit onto the hook. Carefully

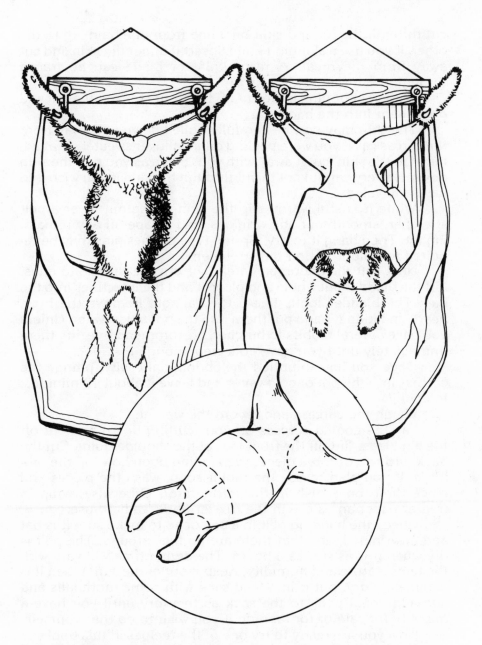

Drawings show three stages of slaughtering, butchering.
Plastic garbage bag is utilized to keep carcass clean
and for disposal of offal.

cut through the fur and skin on a line from one hind leg to the other. If you use a skinning knife, insert it under the skin and cut away from the meat. A razor knife or blade can be traced through the fur and skin.

With your boning knife cut off the front feet and the tail and drop them into the bag.

The skin may now be carefully pulled down and away from the carcass as if you were peeling off a pullover sweater. If fat adheres to the skin, cut it away with your blade as you pull the skin down. Be very careful not to cut through the skin if you wish it to have any value.

While it is still warm, slip the skin inside out, over a pelt stretcher, smooth out any wrinkles, and scrape off any remaining fat. Then hang it to dry. Spring-type clothes pins may be required to hold it flat on the stretcher.

Next, slit the abdomen carefully from breastbone to anus. Lift the bladder out whole and place it and the intestines into the bag. The bladder looks like a toy balloon. Remove the liver, heart, and kidneys and put them into the pot of ice water. Unless you have several rabbits to butcher, I recommend freezing them immediately until you have collected enough for a recipe.

Once you have emptied the abdominal cavity, plunge the carcass into the pot of cold water and leave it about 10 minutes, to cool it.

Weigh the carcass and record the weight.

Lay the cooled carcass on your cutting board and cut off the hind legs. Cut off the front legs at the shoulder joint. Cut the back into two or three pieces, depending upon how big the rabbit is. If you plan to use the rabbit soon, wash the pieces and place them on a dish in the refrigerator. Otherwise, wrap in freezer paper and store in the freezer until ready to use.

Check the hanging pelt in a day or so to make sure it is flat and unwrinkled, and that there are no flies around. The pelt is dry when it is as stiff as a board. The drying time will vary with the temperature and humidity. Keep it out of the sun. When it is completely dry, put it in a feed sack with some mothballs and add additional pelts to the sack as they dry until you have a quantity for sale or for tanning if you wish to do that yourself.

Now you are ready to try one of the recipes in this book, or you may prefer to consult a rabbit cookbook or adapt a favorite chicken or veal recipe.

Chapter 9

Extra Cash for Your Pocket

I began to raise rabbits as a boy to make some extra money. Somewhere I got the notion that I could make quite a bit of cash without much effort.

Since then I have learned that some money can be made with rabbits, but it takes a sizeable effort, and it won't net a great deal of money in most cases.

What rabbits can do very nicely is become the workers in a home factory that requires very little supervision to produce more of themselves, an excellent product for sale, and leave you free to pursue other activities, among them a full-time job. Basically, the rabbits are working day in and day out, and the work required on your part can be accomplished in your spare time, whenever you have it. While you are not likely to make a lot of money with rabbits, that's often also true of other part-time livestock or farming pursuits. What you can make is up to you and depends upon the size of the effort you make and your abilities in marketing and selling, in addition to producing your product. The very best way to sell rabbits is to have rabbits for sale. I know it sounds ridiculous, but of course it isn't.

Many rabbit raisers are reluctant to produce litters because they are afraid they may not be able to dispose of them. I guarantee that if they do not produce them, they will not sell them.

On the other hand, there is some chance that if they do produce them, they will sell them. I have found that I am my own best possible salesman when I have produced a lot of rabbits and have no more hutches in which to keep them. That's when I begin to look around, even to beat the bushes, to make a sale. Necessity drives me to profit.

Here are the opportunities ahead of you:

- **Sale of live or dressed meat rabbits**
- **Sale of live laboratory rabbits**
- **Sale of pet rabbits**
- **Sale of breeding stock**
- **Sale of feed and supplies**
- **Sale of skins**
- **Sale of manure**
- **Manufacture and sale of hutches, nest boxes, and carrying cases.**

It is possible to sell your rabbits and byproducts in all of the above ways. Some raisers use all these selling methods and some stick to one or two. The choice is yours.

Meat Rabbits

If you begin raising rabbits for meat, cooking and enjoying them, it will be a simple matter to tell others how great it tastes. You might begin by inviting relatives or friends for dinner. Your guests are sure to want more of a good thing and you may get an order or two right at the table.

They will want the rabbits butchered and ready for the table. If you are willing to do the work, and you keep your sales limited to family, friends, neighbors, and perhaps co-workers, you will find it a simple routine to butcher your rabbits a litter at a time and prepare them for the freezer—even the freezer compartment of your refrigerator. You can then eat what you like and sell what you don't. Depending upon how many rabbits you raise, your sales can be steady. I'd recommend you keep track of prices in the supermarket and price yours about the same— perhaps a bit lower to offer your customers a bargain. If you raised enough so that you butchered a litter a week, on, perhaps, a Saturday morning, you could make a little extra money.

If you go back to Chapter six where we figured feed costs, you will see that at $11 per hundred, pellet feeding with no cheaper supplements means your cost per pound of dressed meat is 88 cents. Right now rabbit meat sells for about $2.50 per pound. If you sell for $2.50 a pound, your margin over feed costs is $1.62. If you sell eight 2-pounders, which are 8-week New Zealands or 12-week Floridas, your net over feed costs on the eight of them is $25.92. If you did that for a year, say 50 such litters, you would have $1,296 over your feed costs. Of course, by supplementing the pellets you increase your net. Depending upon how resourceful you are, you could double that figure. Of course, you are talking about 400 rabbits. If you sell the dried pelt of each one for 50 cents you increase your annual take another $200.

Butchering eight rabbits every Saturday morning takes some time, although after you are used to doing it you will find you can do the eight in an hour or less. In a commercial processing plant a professional butcher can process 100 per hour.

Finding Buyers

You will also have to take the time to make the transaction and keep the records. Naturally, you have to get the customer. A bulletin board notice at your place of employment might do the trick. A similar notice where other family members are employed might be needed. It's possible to post such notices in other locations, but don't expect the supermarket or corner grocery store to be thrilled with you if suggest it. If you really want to expand your sales, try a classified ad. Use a weekly newspaper that has a lot of classifieds rather than a large daily if you can. The "shopper" papers that are free can be very productive. Club newspapers and bulletins and newsletters can also produce good sales. If there is a local Italian-American Club, or one with French, German, Spanish, Portuguese, or Puerto Rican members, you will be especially fortunate as people of these backgrounds have a tradition of enjoying rabbit meat.

You may wish to sell to restaurants. Doing so can be simpler, because you have fewer customers who buy a greater volume. Usually you can get a retail price, too, although you may want to give the restaurant a price break. Try to deal with expensive French, Italian, and German restaurants if you can.

Call the owner or the chef and ask if you can discuss your rabbit meat with him. Invite him to see your rabbitry to inspect it for cleanliness. Give him a free rabbit or two to try. He may want it fresh and not frozen, so make your arrangements accordingly. The chef may want to cut up the carcass himself (in fact, he may want to do the butchering himself). You may need a license from your state for such sales.

It's A Delicacy

You may also need a license to sell to stores. If you go in for this business, you will have to sell at wholesale prices. Position your rabbit meat as a specialty, a delicacy, and try to get the best possible price, but remember if a store buys in quantity it will want to get a good deal. It will be looking for a 50 to 100 percent markup. The benefit to you in such an arrangement will lie in quantity sales. While your margin per rabbit will not be as great as with direct sales or restaurant sales, the volume may make it worth your while, and you will save time.

The way to save time with rabbit meat sales is to sell to a processor, or a broker who supplies a processor. Almost every area of the country has such a person in business. You can locate one in your locale by inquiries at the feed store or the rabbit club. Some processors or brokers will pick up your rabbits. Others want you to deliver. Most want them to weigh 4–6 pounds and lately they have been paying from 60 cents to $1 a pound live weight. It costs you at most 44 cents for the feed to produce a pound, so you can see you won't make much on this arrangement, but it won't take you much time, either. No butchering, wrapping, freezing. It can leave you time to sell rabbits in other ways.

Laboratory Sales

In some areas of the country there is a good market for laboratory rabbits. If you live near a large medical center or university, pharmaceutical company, or government laboratory such as those of the Food and Drug Administration and its consultants and contractors, you may contact them with an offer of laboratory rabbits. Ordinarily they will want white rabbits. If you raise New Zealands or Floridas, you will have what they want.

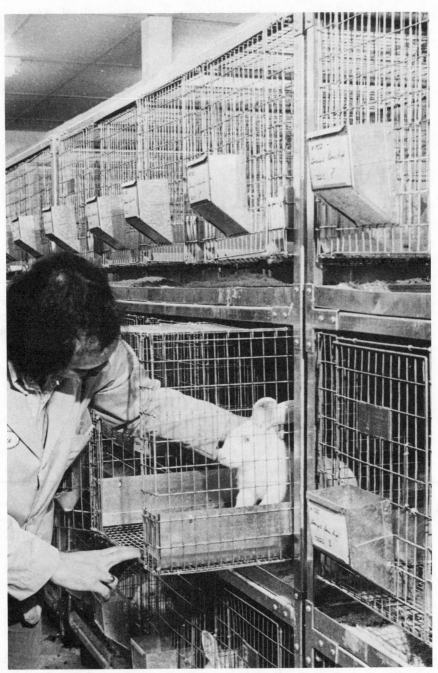

New Zealand Whites in laboratory cages.

Laboratory payment varies greatly. If you sell direct to the lab you will get the most money, and it usually is considerably more than what you can get for meat rabbits. The problem is one of being able to supply just what the lab needs when the lab needs it. For example, it may want a quantity of females 4 months of age. You may not have such a quantity. And if you do, you will still have to do something with the rest of the stock available for sale.

That's why most rabbit raisers who sell laboratory stock also sell to a broker much like the meat broker and, in fact, often the same person. You have some of the does and other rabbit raisers have the rest. It is up to the broker to gather them up and deliver them to the lab. The broker won't pay you as much as the lab because he will be making a profit. On the other hand, you should receive more than you get for meat rabbits.

The way to sell lab rabbits (or any other kind of rabbits or just about anything else) is to take the direct approach. Identify the buyer and tell him what you have to offer. Don't be put off by the notion that he may have all he needs or that a newcomer can't break in with him. Labs and brokers are always looking for **reliable** suppliers of **healthy** rabbits. If you are such a supplier, you can rest assured you will have a market for your rabbits.

Pet Rabbit Sales

Here's a sales category I'm not really thrilled with, but everybody inquires about it, and it is possible to turn a dollar selling pet rabbits. First of all, if you sell somebody a pet rabbit, you are going to have the devil of a time selling him a meat rabbit. Who wants to eat his pet? You might sell a person one pet rabbit in a lifetime. You might sell him one meat rabbit a week.

I'd like to warn you not to sell pets direct to individuals. I've done that myself and it is not worth the grief that you encounter, unless you sell a complete package that includes the rabbit, feed, hutch, feeder, and water bottle or crock, and complete, written instructions for care. If you do this, you may place classified ads in local papers. Do not put prices in your ads, but limit them to something vague like "Adorable baby bunnies for sale." When people phone, arrange to have them visit you at a convenient time. After they have picked up and petted the adorable rabbit, tell them the price tag. Also tell them the rabbit is for sale only with the hutch, feed, and instructions. Instructions

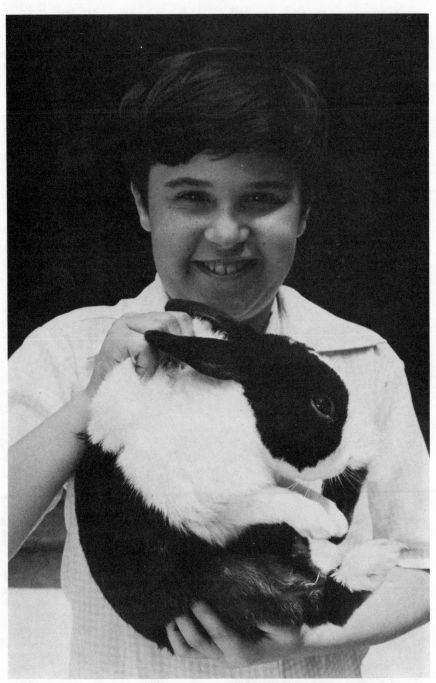

A pet Black Dutch being picked up properly.

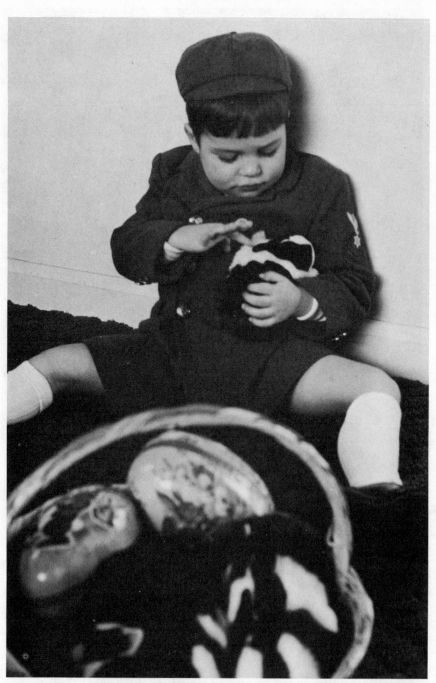

All dressed up on Easter Sunday with a basket of Dutch bunnies.

A pet Champagne D'Argent rabbit.

may be written up by you and given away, or they might be in the form of a book you will sell (I recommend my own, naturally, **The T.F.H. Book of Pet Rabbits**). Compare pet store and feed store prices to set your price.

Sell feed in a 10-pound bag, weighed from the 50- or 100-pound bags you buy for your own rabbits. Double the price you paid per pound.

The idea here is to send the rabbit owner home with everything he needs to keep this pet alive and well for the benefit and enjoyment of both rabbit and owner. And yourself. If you don't equip this new owner completely, you will regret it. First of all, you cannot be assured that the rabbit has a secure and comfortable home. Second, you don't know what it will be fed. Third, you don't know how it will be handled. Fourth, after it has been mis-housed, mis-fed and abused, it will become ill or even die and you will regret the phone call you will receive from the ill-prepared purchaser who is both unhappy and demanding his money back. If you heed any advice in this book at all, make sure it is the above. Don't say I didn't warn you.

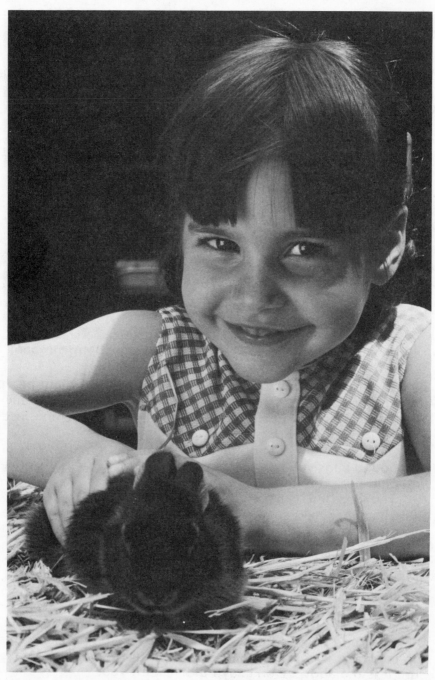

A baby Tan rabbit is a cute pet.

The truth is that with hutch and feed sales, by buying books and marking them up, you can pocket quite a bit per pet rabbit sale. Say $10 for the rabbit and $10 profit on the hutch. Another $3 on the book and a dollar or so on the feed. Twenty-four dollars per rabbit sold on the profit side is not bad. Anything less, if it does not include the equipment and information, is a bad deal as far as I'm concerned.

You can sell pet rabbits to pet stores and you can make it pay. The best time of year is just before Easter, as far as demand is concerned. All the talk about the Easter bunny fuels the flames of desire among youngsters for a pet rabbit.

I don't recommend selling to the pet stores, but I'll tell you how to do it. I used to do it myself, but I haven't for years.

In the springtime, and perhaps throughout the year, especially at Chistmas time, pet stores will have a demand for rabbits. They will sell them at prices of $10 to $50 each, depending upon the neighborhood and the type of rabbit. White rabbits won't bring much. The big demand is in Dwarfs and Lops. Fancy stores will bring the best prices. The pet stores will mark up the rabbits 100 to 200 percent, so you might received only $2 or $3 or as much as $25 for a pet from a store.

They might pay you outright or want to put them on consignment. Consignment is not really a bad deal. You still own the rabbit. If the store doesn't have an order for it and you do, you can take it back and sell it yourself. Make sure you and the pet store manager have a clear understanding of your agreement ahead of time, including how much you are to be paid, when you will deliver, and whether you can (or must) take the rabbit back if it is not sold.

Breeding Stock Sales

As you become more proficient at raising rabbits you will find yourself in for the best deal of all in terms of sales and profit from a small, backyard, part-time rabbit operation. That's selling breeding stock.

The key to this lies in first obtaining quality animals from a good breeder. Rabbits with pedigree papers are essential.

If you obtain good quality animals yourself, there is absolutely no reason why you can't receive for them the same price you paid. That is, you should ask and receive for the rabbits you produce a price comparable to what you paid for their parents.

Many, many rabbit raisers recover the cost of the original breeding pair when they produce their first litter.

As you raise that first litter, friends and co-workers will learn of your success. They will want to visit your budding rabbitry and learn of your goals. No matter why you raise rabbits, for meat, lab, breeding stock—even pets—you doubtless will find among your circle of acquaintances a number of people who will wish to follow your lead. Rabbit raising definitely is a growth situation. In the past 20 years the number of people raising rabbits has increased by more than 500 percent. The American Rabbit Breeders Association membership has risen from 8,000 to 35,000 in that period and that membership represents only a small part of the breeders. The nation's largest feed manufacturer, Ralston Purina, revealed recently that rabbit feed is its fastest growing specialty feed. That means rabbit feed sales have increased faster than that of poultry and even of dogs and cats.

If you start out with just a few rabbits, but good quality specimens, you will find it difficult not to sell breeders. If you add more, you can begin to advertise. I have recommended for years that anyone beginning with breeding stock should start with at least two bucks and two does. With two pairs to breed from, your customers will have two litters of "unrelated" (not a brother-sister breeding pair) rabbits to choose from to form their own breeding pairs or trios. A pair or a trio is enough to get them started raising meat and laboratory stock. For further production of a breeding stock herd, they will want two pairs themselves.

Advertise

You can increase your sales of breeding stock locally by putting up notices at area feed stores. Do not be bashful about this; the stores will welcome such advertisements. The more rabbits there are, the more feed they sell. Try buying some business cards. Leave a supply with every feed dealer in the area. Invite phone calls for appointments to inspect your stock. Be ready to show the pedigree papers as well as the rabbits to prospective buyers. If the rabbit supply exceeds the demand, branch out by advertising in the pennysaver shopper newspapers, the weeklies, and even the dailies. If you join a local rabbit club you will find other members interested in your stock.

Author ships rabbits across the country by air in these wirebound vegetable crates.

Showing your rabbits may hold appeal; it will promote sales. Breeding stock sales offer the highest unit return for your animals. Many rabbit raisers make a nice second income from sales locally and some even offer them through advertisements in national rabbit publications, such as **Domestic Rabbits** magazine. They receive orders in the mail and ship the rabbits by air. I have been doing this for nearly 20 years. It is a simple matter to make arrangements at your nearest airport. Rabbits ship safely across the country and even around the world. Your airline can advise you on crating and other shipping requirements. The airlines are happy to do this because it's their business—a good percentage of their income comes from the air freight business, and live animals are a surprisingly large share of that.

Sale of Feed and Supplies

Once you begin to have visitors to your rabbitry, and make a few sales of either pet or breeding rabbits, you have the opportunity to sell feed and such supplies and equipment as crocks and feeders, even nest boxes and hutches. A pet rabbit buyer may not wish to buy feed by the 50-pound sack, but prefer to purchase 5 or 10 pounds at a time. You can weigh it out and bag it up from your own feed sacks, and you should double your price per pound for the trouble. Should you decide to order

Tanned pelt (left) and dried pelts on drying frames are held by Tony Pisanelli.

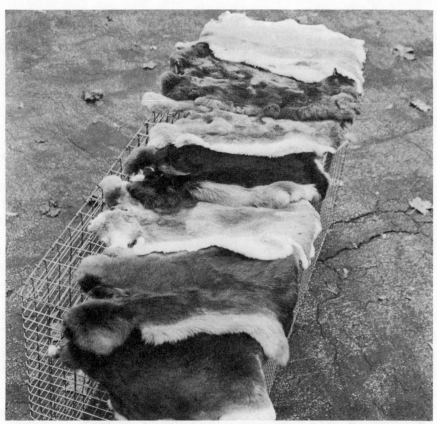

A variety of tanned pelts from several kinds of rabbits.

feeders, nest boxes, hutch wire, or hutches from a mailorder house inquire about wholesale prices. If you buy in quantity you can receive a price that will allow you to resell at a profit. If your local store does not stock equipment, put up a notice of your supplies for sale in the store. Do not expect to do this if such items are available there, of course.

If you decide to get into hutch building, you may purchase wire, clips, and pliers locally and build hutches for your rabbit customers. I find it profitable and efficient to build standard size hutches and have them available for all customers. By standardizing on size, I have a smooth manufacturing routine. If a customer wants special sizes or configurations, and some people do to fit in a shed or some other specific location, you may want to fill the need. If so, you should price such hutches higher (unless they are significantly smaller than the norm) based on the material and the time it takes for construction. Also, get paid in advance. Nobody else wants the odd sizes.

Other Sales

We have mentioned the sale of skins and manure already, but they are worth repeating because they do represent the potential for additional income. You may wish to learn to tan your pelts. I recommend a good book on the subject in the back of this one. If you do, you or someone in your family may wind up producing mittens, slippers, stuffed toys, collars, cuffs or other items for still another potential sideline.

If you are a gardener you may not wish to part with your manure. I know some people who raise rabbits **primarily** for the manure, which does not burn plants even when applied fresh, and which has a higher nitrogen content than most animal manures. It is amazing stuff and it will do wonders for your landscape, applied to flowers, vegetables, shrubs, and trees—even the lawn. It will do the same for others, of course, so you may prefer to sell it. Take a look at what dried cow manure is selling for at the garden center. Price rabbit manure higher and put it on consignment there. Fork it right into the bag that came from the feed store, mark it plainly with the name of its contents, put it on display in the spring and the fall, and get ready to reap the profits.

Your rewards in selling are related to your ability as a marketer and sales person, to be sure, but with good rabbits at your place you will find several ways to add cash to your pocket.

Chapter 10

Rabbit Shows—
Recreation with Rabbits

If you raise rabbits mainly for meat, fur, laboratory, or even as pets, you should consider producing them for a secondary reason as well. It is the primary purpose for thousands of breeders.

Show!

While all raisers know how versatile rabbits are, more and more are learning that they have a double identity, too. That's because every rabbit, regardless of its utilitarian or commercial attributes, also becomes a show specimen as soon as its hocks hit a judging table.

That's right. Every rabbit that goes to a show is a show rabbit. So if you have pedigreed, purebred rabbits, you are already equipped with potential show stock. If not, you should have some, because if you do, you will become more successful as a breeder of meat, laboratory, pet, or breeding stock. Purebred stock is readily available and inexpensive.

A purebred rabbit is one bred to a certain written physical description, called a standard. Purebreds are also called standardbred or thoroughbred and these terms are nearly synonymous with another used to describe them—pedigreed. This purebred rabbit has a written record of its ancestry—a pedigree —as evidence of its pure breeding.

All this can mean a lot to a rabbit breeder, even if his primary objective is to produce meat for his own or someone else's table. The breeder of New Zealand Whites, for example, will find that a total of 55 points out of 100 is allotted by the judge to **body type.** He will look for broad and smooth hindquarters, a broad, firm, and meaty back, and firm, well-developed shoulders, among other things. These attributes, of course, are exactly what the meat producer should seek if he wants to produce the most meat possible on a New Zealand with the least amount of feed and in the shortest possible time.

The judge will also examine the New Zealand's fur, looking for precisely what makes the pelt most valuable to the furrier. A rabbit producer who overlooks the importance of the pelt may as well raise chickens.

Where the Money Is

At the same time, there is the matter of breeding stock sales. Every meat rabbit producer sells some breeding stock at one time or another, even if he isn't trying. The fact that you can supply pedigree papers and that your stock conforms with the standard for your breed will only increase the return you can expect from breeding stock sales. And for the small raiser, this is really where the money is in rabbit raising.

Showing rabbits costs very little, and it's a lot of fun for the entire family. Many combine showing with sightseeing, tailgate picnics, and even fishing trips. At the show, there's the chance to meet other breeders and talk shop, an opportunity to sell some of your rabbits or buy someone else's. Probably most important is getting the judge's opinion, and making your own comparisons of your rabbits and those of others at the show.

What It's All About

Not to be overlooked is the chance to meet new friends with whom you can enjoy the competition. This competition is never of the fairly brutal sort found at dog and horse shows. I have attended fancy horse shows in exclusive suburban areas of the country and big league dog shows in Madison Square Garden in New York. At none of them have I found the fine competitors and the true sportsmanship I've encountered at rabbit shows throughout the United States. Rabbit people are a fine class of people!

Scene at a typical rabbit show.

And competition is most of what it's all about. If you have watched young rabbits grow daily for several months in anticipation of a show, and then thrilled to their victory before your fellow breeders who have been nurturing their own hopes, you have enjoyed an experience not at all unlike that of the builder of an Indianapolis 500-winning car or even the owner of a Kentucky Derby-winning horse.

Beyond that, no matter why you raise rabbits, you will raise better ones after attending a few shows. At the outset, you will learn, better than any other way, the important features of your chosen breed. And by continued showing you will stay abreast (perhaps ahead) of the progress being made by producers of your breed.

One Thousand Shows

Finding shows is easy. Nearly 1,000 such events take place each year in the United States. These are sanctioned by the American Rabbit Breeders Association and, in most cases, also by breed clubs. I'll elaborate a little later on the implications of the term "sanction," but for now you should know that a sanctioned show is what we are talking about in this book. That's an event that is sponsored by one of the nation's 350 local and state specialty rabbit clubs, 100 state associations, 30 national associations, 60 youth clubs, or 65 fairs, under the jurisdiction of the ARBA. We are not including such events as 4-H shows, most of which operate exclusively for the benefit of children, and under another set of rules.

These shows take place from coast to coast in the United States and Canada. Recently they have begun in Puerto Rico.

Most shows are one-day affairs and occur in the spring or fall, with each sponsoring club holding one or two or more per year. Fair shows usually take place in late summer, and often last several days or a week.

A Thousand Rabbits

Local and state association shows include all recognized breeds. National specialty clubs, which sponsor individual breeds, usually stage annual shows exclusively for their breed, often in conjunction with a local or state association show. Regional single-breed shows also take place. Ordinarily, a few hundred to a thousand rabbits are on exhibit at these events.

All rabbit shows are put on by volunteer members of the sponsoring club. Nobody gets paid except the judges, who earn their licenses to serve after an apprenticeship and study of ARBA procedures and successful completion of rigorous examination. Judging usually begins early on a Sunday morning and continues through the day until all the breeds are judged. Shows also feature refreshments, displays of rabbitry equipment, rows of crates of rabbits for sale, and considerable discussion and evaluation of this stock. For the most part, the prizes are modest sums of money, armfuls of brilliantly colored ribbons and rosettes, and a score or more of glittering trophies. There are other important things to be won, such as "points" and "legs," and I'll go into that soon. In the meantime, you should know about the additional fun to be had.

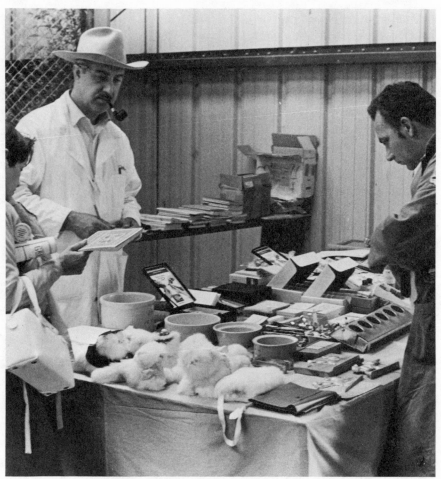

Exhibitors look over supplies for sale at rabbit show.

The Biggest Show of the Year

All of this local activity culminates in, and necessarily is overshadowed by, the biggest show of the year, that which is held in conjunction with the annual convention of the ARBA. This show, generally referred to simply as the "national convention," moves to a different location each year, usually near a major metropolitan area. Breeders drive or fly in from all parts of the country, often saving their vacation for the show, which lasts most of a week. If they can't go themselves, they ship their rabbits in by air.

Trophies and rosette ribbons await winners at show.

In addition to the judging, the national convention includes a trade show where suppliers of equipment display their wares, and leaders of breed associations promote the rabbit varieties they love best. It's a time to catch up on the latest information in the rabbit world and to renew old acquaintances. One breeder I know has attended every ARBA Convention without fail for the past 35 years! There are sightseeing tours, banquets, a ball, parties, and meetings of the officers and members of the breed clubs and the ARBA itself. And it all gets bigger and better every year.

Looking at a rabbit show from a strictly monetary standpoint, there are several things to consider. First of all, for each rabbit you enter, you pay an entry fee of $1.25 to $2 at a local show and up to $5 at a national convention.

'Specials' Provide More Fun

Where's all the cash you will win? In most shows, you won't win much. Of course, that's really a good thing in a way. It probably does more to keep rabbit shows friendly and honest than anything else.

And yet, there is some cash to be won. Usually, it's in the form of "specials," which are cash donations put up by breeders, ordinarily on their own breed, as a challenge and an incentive to other exhibitors. This may be as little as a dollar or two on a class winner, but it all makes showing that much more fun. When the breeders support their own breed with specials, the competition improves. Specials not only provide prize money, they also offer publicity for the breeders who put them up.

Several years ago my favorite breed, the Tan, was rather obscure and few were exhibited. I'd go to a show and mine would be the only ones there; or perhaps one or two other breeders would be there and we'd exhibit a grand total of maybe a dozen animals.

When a few of us decided to put up generous specials, we soon attracted so many new breeders that we now have one of the largest entries at eastern shows, if not nationally. I have found it makes a lot of sense for me, as a major breeder, to put up $10 or $15 or more in specials. Sometimes I offer other awards (as do several other breeders) such as silver serving sets, copies of my books, or some useful item for the rabbitry. Many others offer only a few dollars in this breed but have other breeds as well, so they spread their money around. The main thing to remember is that it all adds up, what with hundreds of exhibitors at a show, and soon the specials amount to something pretty good.

More Money Can Be Yours

At a county or state fair show, where the rabbit entries are subsidized by the state agriculture department, you are likely to find a "payback" in addition to specials. You will also receive a payback at a national convention and at a few other shows where the club has been able to raise enough money to afford it.

The payback is based on the number of rabbits entered in a particular class. First place might pay but a dollar or two if only three or four rabbits are entered in it, or as much as $15 with fifty entered. There also is money for second, third, fourth, and fifth place winners, and even further back in the pack in some shows.

Trophies, ribbons, checks, grand championship "legs" can be won at shows.

In most shows, however, you probably will do well to recover your entry fee from the payback. Let's say you enter half a dozen rabbits at $1.50 each. You've invested $9 in entry fees. Even if you are the big winner for your breed, you may not win more than the $9.

A fair show that is the beneficiary of a subsidy often will be well worth winning as far as money alone is concerned. I know several topnotch breeders who profit by $100 or more at fair shows each year.

Where It Really Pays Off

Of course, in addition to the cash, the rosettes, and the ribbons, there is **reputation**. If you are a winner, you will find increased demand for your stock, and at higher prices. Certainly, others also want to win and once they find out you are a winner in your breed, you will have no trouble selling them your excess stock at fancy prices.

So you can see that if you are a consistent winner, you will never have to worry about paying for the feed. To the really dedicated fancier, however, there are two things worth more than trophies, ribbons, or even money. The first is "legs."

A "leg" is more correctly called a "Record of Leg of Grand Champion Certificate." Three of these certificates must be won by a single rabbit before it can be a grand champion. Having a grand champion in your rabbitry is like having a Rolls Royce in your garage. It's class, but it's not easy.

To win one leg certificate, a rabbit must do one of the following:

1. Win first in a class of not less than five entries owned by three or more exhibitors.

2. Win Best of Breed provided there are five or more shown in the breed by three or more exhibitors.

3. Win Best Opposite Sex of Breed provided there are five or more shown in the breed with three or more exhibitors.

4. Win Best of Variety provided there are five or more of the same sex as the winner shown in the variety with three or more exhibitors.

5. Win Best Opposite Sex of Variety provided there are five or more of the same sex as the winner shown in the variety with three or more exhibitors.

6. Win Best of Show.

No more than one leg can be won in a single show with the same animal. To become a grand champion, the rabbit must win legs under at least two ARBA judges, at least one leg as an intermediate or a senior. Of course, each leg must be won in an ARBA-sanctioned show and under an ARBA judge.

Certificates of Achievement

Once a rabbit has won three legs under the above conditions, the legs can be sent to ARBA headquarters, with the rabbit's registration number and a $2 fee, and a Grand Champion

A Black Tan.

Certificate will be awarded. If your rabbit wins Best in Show, it may also receive a handsome certificate for a similar fee.

Once the word gets around that you have produced a grand champion, or even better that you have some of its offspring for sale, you will have no trouble in commanding fancy prizes for your fancy rabbits. That's rather worth winning.

But there's more—another intangible that can add to your reputation and to the value of your rabbits. That's "sweepstakes points." Sweepstakes points are awarded by breed clubs for various placings in shows, provided the show is sanctioned by the breed clubs. A while back I mentioned sanction fees paid by the local club, which uses the money to pay a secretary to record points and also to award special ribbons, rosettes, and sweepstakes trophies.

Here's the way the sweepstakes works:

Each of the major recognized breeds is sponsored by a breed association, such as the American Tan Rabbit Specialty Club or the American Federation of New Zealand Breeders. There are more than thirty such organizations in the United States.

How Points Are Awarded

Each club has a secretary. One of the secretary's tasks is to keep track of the winnings of members in the various local and other types of shows throughout the year. Depending on placings and the number of rabbits in that breed entered, the secretary assigns points to each member, according to the following schedule:

First place, six times the number of entries in the class.
Second place, four times the number of entries in the class.
Third place, three times the number of entries.
Fourth place, two times.
And Fifth place, one times.

If you have won first place, for example, with five rabbits in the class, you would have thirty points. In another class you might win third out of ten, and get another thirty points.

You pay an annual membership fee to the specialty club, and, among other things, you are entitled to have your points counted. The local club sponsoring the show pays the sanction fee to each specialty club, mainly to attract you as an exhibitor. To explain how well this works, I, like many others, wouldn't be bothered showing my rabbits in a show that didn't have a sanction for my breed, because I wouldn't get any points.

Why do I want the points? Well, they are added up, throughout the year, and prizes are awarded to those who amass the most points in the year.

Comparing Your Winnings

The sweepstakes race is reported throughout the year in the club newsletter along with reports of the shows from coast to coast, so a breeder can see how his winning record compares with that of fellow members.

What does the sweepstakes prove? That's a matter of some debate. Does the winner have the best rabbits of his breed? Not necessarily. Winning the sweepstakes race proves that you have good rabbits, which win consistently, and that you attend **a lot of shows**. But it's not possible for some breeders to attend more than a few shows each year. Perhaps they are geographically isolated, or they may simply not be able to get to shows because of conflicts due to employment or family activities. But the sweepstakes race does tend to encourage showing as frequently as possible, and that makes for more competition for everyone.

The Big Prize for Me

You can see from all of this that while showing rabbits takes only a small investment, it doesn't return very much in prize money. In fact, if you consider only the prize money you receive from the show secretaries, it probably will cost you in the long run. But I don't know how to have more fun, more pure sport and entertainment for a whole family on less money. And there's no denying it, being a winner makes all your rabbits that much more in demand.

In the final analysis, though, the big prize for me is **satisfaction**. It's the old "virtue being it's own best reward" thing. When I come in a winner, I'm just so darned pleased with myself as a breeder, conditioner and exhibitor that I take even more pride and pure satisfaction in my rabbits than ever before.

To be sure, I like to win the money, the ribbons, the rosettes, the trophies, the legs, and the points. But I'd still show if they gave me none of those. I'd settle for the judge's nod.

The Best Breed?

When you come right down to it, most breeders choose the rabbit that appeals most to them. They simply like that breed best. They may or may not have good reasons, and they really don't care. They are breeding and showing rabbits for the fun of it and they want the breed they like best. And who can argue with them?

The one who can argue is the one who calculates his chances of winning. He isn't like "most breeders," for, in fact, most breeders do **not** win consistently. The consistent winner has thought about the situation just a bit more. He gives some

Winners flank judge and winning rabbit at show.

A Champagne D'Argent, another excellent meat rabbit.

thought to what appeals to him, but also to some practical considerations. These include **the chance to win, the breeding challenge**, and **the degree of competition**. Less significant, but also practical considerations, are the size of the rabbit, size of the herd, and such points as ease of management and housing.

There are many different kinds of rabbits; probably too many. Hardly a year goes by but that a new breed or variety makes its debut. Within these breeds are many more varieties, and it surely is not possible, or even desirable, to raise them all. There are thirteen varieties of Rex, for example, and five "groups" of Netherland Dwarfs comprising more than twenty varieties. Anyone who tried to raise all of them probably would have to devote seven days a week to it and employ a full-time staff of pedigree researchers.

As a rabbit exhibitor, you might narrow your choice by saying you will show only a "fancy" breed. There have been many discussions, and even heated arguments, about what constitutes a fancy breed and what is a commercial rabbit. The ARBA Standards Committee has even come out with guidelines in which it classifies twenty-four breeds as fancy and a dozen as commercial. These classifications are useful when a judge wants to choose Best in Show winners from each category, but that's about as far as it goes. Try to tell the man who makes his living selling Dutch to laboratories that his rabbit is not commercial and he'll laugh at you. To me, any rabbit on a judging table is "fancy." And any rabbit that turns a profit is "commercial."

Consider the Competition

Let's look at rabbits from an important standpoint—competition. Victory without competition is hollow, indeed. If you are ready for stiff competition, you'll find it in such breeds as New Zealand, Satin, Netherland Dwarf, Dutch, and Rex. How about a moderate amount? Then consider Florida Whites, Californians, Champagnes, English Spots, Flemish Giants, Polish, Palominos, Chinchillas, Checkered Giants, Silver Martens, French Lops, or Tans.

In any of the above breeds you will be going head to head with the nation's top breeders. Should you win against them, victory will be sweet.

On the other hand, if you choose a more obscure breed and work with it a while, you may be able to popularize it and get

English Spot.

ahead of the pack, all the while selling breeding stock to increase the competition. That opportunity is available in Americans, Alaskas, Belgians, Beverens, Blue Viennas, Himalayans, Harlequins, or the up-and-coming Cinnamons and Britannia Petites.

While the above generalizations about popularity may be made on a national basis, there are regional differences. In some parts of the country some moderately popular breeds nationally are rarely shown.

Of course, you will have a lot more fun if there's fairly strong competition. Beating yourself is not really rewarding. If you do have your heart set on a little-shown breed, perhaps with the intent of leading the way to its popularity, you might also show a more popular breed at the same time.

One or Two Breeds Is Enough

You should limit your show herd to one or two breeds only, so that you will have the time and space needed to become successful with them. Too many fanciers try to be a jack-of-all-breeds, with the obvious result that they master none.

Breeding Challenge—Top Consideration

Winning a show is, of course, only the culmination of meeting the breeding challenge. How much of a challenge can you handle? A solid-colored or white rabbit, in my opinion, does not offer nearly the challenge of a marked animal. When you breed a white or solid-colored animal, you don't have to consider markings, and you are likely to produce more specimens that are good representatives of the breed. I would rate marked rabbits as most challenging. Next come such breeds as Chinchillas, Silvers, and Champagnes where the hair shaft coloring is extremely important to the overall look of the animal. They are followed by the solid-colored rabbits and, last, the whites.

This is a very controversial viewpoint, I realize. There are those New Zealand and Florida white breeders, for example, who absolutely can see several colors of white on a single judge's table. Beyond that, the competition in New Zealands, Satins, and some other solid-colored rabbits is so fierce that slight nuances of fur quality and type become extremely important.

Marked Breeds Have It All

Nevertheless, in the long run, all the considerations of the solid-colored and white rabbits are present in the marked breeds, but the markings are there as well, and there are at least two colors to contend with in a single rabbit. Each of these markings has its faint differences, too. Don't expect to convince a diehard Satin breeder with this argument, however.

While in all marked breeds you have the same challenges of the solid, or the agouti (those with bands of color on the hair shafts), not all of them offer the same breeding challenge. In Dutch, for example, a lot of luck is involved because so many of the rabbits born are disqualified from showing because of mismarkings that the breeder really can't control. In addition, most marked breeds feature an animal that is one color plus white. I'm thinking of Checkered Giants, English Spots, and Dutch. My favorite breed, however, offers two body colors. That's the Tan.

I'd like to explain, using the Tan as an example, what's involved in breeding and showing a marked rabbit. The Tan comes in four varieties—Black, Blue, Chocolate, and Lilac. These are the topside body colors. The undercolor of each is tan. When you breed and show Tans, you are creating a chal-

A trio of young Tans.

lenge for yourself with more parts of the animal than in any other breed. There is type, of course, and fur and condition.

But then there are two different colors, and there are areas where these colors should be and where they should not. You will practically never have a Tan disqualified because of a mismarking, however, as often is the case with the Dutch. On the plus side, you can, in fact, produce Tans with excellent markings because of your own good breeding practices in selecting the right pair to mate. You can **breed for** markings, and that adds to the fun and satisfaction.

I realize, of course, that my fondness for the Tan can be viewed as subjective, because, after all, there are 100 points to be considered in every single breed, and to appreciate the challenge of many breeds you simply have to breed them.

Size of the Rabbit and the Herd

When calculating your chance to win, considering the competition and the breeding challenge, don't forget something else: when planning a show herd, size is important. Size of the individual rabbit and size of the whole herd. If you choose a large rabbit, you will need large cages and a lot of feed. A small rabbit obviously has some advantages here. Cages are smaller, appetites are smaller, and overall space required for a given number is smaller. If you are planning only a show herd, you may want to decide on a small breed for these reasons.

Just a Few Will Do

How many rabbits must you maintain to produce winners? The longer you raise them and the better you get at it, the fewer you need. That's because you get to be a better judge of your own stock and learn to predict what it will do for you.

Some of the best breeders in the country have no more than a dozen or so breeding does. They do keep more bucks than is "necessary" for production. Ask a meat producer how many bucks he needs and he'll probably say one for every ten or twelve does. But a show rabbit raiser needs more. The thing to remember here is that you are not simply **producing** rabbits or **raising** rabbits when you set out to win the shows. You have to become a rabbit **breeder** and you have to maintain enough breeding combinations to let you earn that name.

Silver Fox.

Should you add breeds or go into breeds with many varieties, your need for breeders, hutch space, and **time** will increase. With few exceptions, the big winners year after year are those who stick to one breed—or only a couple at the most. And they don't have so many rabbits that they can't give them enough attention to learn what they need to know to win.

If you want to win rabbit shows, the only place to get your breeding stock is from a winner. There simply is no sense fooling around with any other source. Not beginners. Not kids. No bargains. Don't plan to buy cheap stock and "upgrade" it. Start with the very best you can find. It will be far cheaper in the long run. When you start right, you have to start only once.

Before you spend a nickel for a rabbit, spend a few dollars to join the specialty club of your chosen breed. See who's winning the sweepstakes. Determine the top breeders of that breed. Get the club newsletter and it won't be long before you'll know where to go for good rabbits. Maybe it will be close to home, and, if so, the task of getting good rabbits will be easier. If not, don't despair. You can get excellent stock shipped to you.

You may have to write a few letters to several of the top breeders before you make up your mind. Don't be in a big rush to buy the first rabbits you hear about. Evaluate the replies you get from these top breeders to see what they have available. Some don't have much for sale.

Look for Productivity

I like to buy from a breeder who not only is a top producer of fine specimens of his breed, but who breeds enough of them so that you know his rabbits are productive as well as beautiful. My ideal breeder is the one who breeds them all year round and sells a lot of his stock to other breeders. If he breeds all the time, you know his rabbits are producers. If he sells all the time, you know his rabbits are in demand. And if he wins more than his share of trophies, you can be sure that his customers will win more than their share, too.

What's extremely important about buying your breeding stock is to remember that you are not merely buying a few animals. You are purchasing all the years of experience in breeding and showing that the owner has been able to give them. If he has been breeding and showing winners for many years, you are buying the sum total of all his knowledge and efforts, up to now.

It isn't just what these rabbits are in themselves, it's also what their ancestors have been and what their descendants will be. They must have been bred with winning in mind for years.

Four Rabbits Make a Good Start

Two junior bucks, a junior doe, and a bred senior doe make an ideal start. This way you get something to raise and grow, something to show, and a litter on the way for next season's shows, all at the same time. But, most important, you have a sound basis for starting your own herd. By the following year you can easily have 100 rabbits, and those would be only the best of the bunch.

Pairs To Sell

Unless you are overloaded with cash, do not order show winners, because, even if a seller parts with them, it will prove only that you have money. Instead, ask him to select the three juniors that he feels will go best with each other from a breeding standpoint. Then tell him you would like the senior doe to be the one that he has been pleased with but would be willing to let go because either he already has what he wants out of her, because he needs to make room for a promising youngster, or even because her breeding career is on the wane. You may have to point this out to him to get him to part with her.

How You Know the Stock Is Good

Because this breeder is a consistent winner, his untried juniors are bound to hold promise. Their parents doubtless have winning records. Chances are their sires, at least, are grand champions. And his senior doe, if she has hung around his rabbitry for a year or two, is certain to be valuable as a productive breeder.

Otherwise, you can be sure, she would not have lasted so long in his rabbitry. He has kept her because she has good ancestry, progressed well herself, and proved herself as a breeder. If she's a year or two old, her offspring have been good, or she wouldn't still be there.

The young prove the parents. That's another way of saying that the true test of a breeding pair is their offspring. A pair of breeders becomes a good pair only when their youngsters are good. And this doe wouldn't still be there if her youngsters weren't good. Not if you are buying from the right person. A winner.

There is one indispensable book you must acquire no matter which breed or breeds you choose to raise. And there is one additional book you must get for each of these breeds. And then, there are three major keys to success.

The first book is the **Standard of Perfection**. The second is the guide book for your particular breed.

The **Standard of Perfection** contains complete standards for all those breeds recognized by the ARBA and which can be entered in ARBA shows.

The **Standard of Perfection** contains 127 pages, seventy-three illustrations, and all the specifications, with point allotments, by which rabbits are judged in ARBA shows. It provides, for each breed, the descriptions of the required size, shape, color, weight, etc., for ideal specimens that have no disqualifications that would bar them from registration by the ARBA.

Experienced breeders have written the standards, which they revise every five years as a committee appointed by the ARBA president. They make changes only for the good of the breed.

The individual breed standards are arranged to present the various sections for consideration in as uniform a method as possible. Type, weight, and condition are placed first, followed by fur, color, markings, head, and ears. Judges are supposed to consider each section when making comparative evaluations of rabbits on the show table, or assess each animal in comparison to the ideal. Judging should in all cases be done by comparison to the standard, and to each other animal on the table.

In addition to offering a complete written physical description of the ideal specimen of each breed for the breeder and for the judge who uses the **Standard of Perfection** when he judges each breed, the book contains much other information that you shouldn't be without if you are going to be a winner.

Jargon, Rules Included

There is a very extensive glossary of terms used to describe rabbits and their attributes or faults. It tells you exactly what is meant by agouti, glaze, bowed legs, broken coat, butterfly, guard hair, luster, pinched hips, snipey, and wry tail in addition to more than 300 other terms that you must know if you are to be a successful exhibitor of rabbits.

It includes show rules—what you can and cannot do when showing your rabbits. Excellent photos of proper posing, handling, and examination during judging are included; articles on what is sought in both commercial and Rex fur and a listing of ideal and registration weights for each breed are important features. Descriptions of fur classes and fur standards for all breeds are covered. Rules governing awards; faults, eliminations, disqualifications; a guide for judging meat classes, and requirements for admitting new breeds to the standards are also included.

This information is followed by the standard for each breed. Depending upon the number of varieties which must be described in each breed, these standards run from one to several pages.

Second Indispensable Book

The second book you must have is the guide book for your chosen breed. This book comes at no extra charge when you join the club that sponsors your breed. A listing of these clubs and their membership fees are contained in the ARBA yearbook, which ARBA members receive free.

Each breed club either has a guide book or has one in production. Membership in the breed club is essential, of course, to the fullest enjoyment of the breed, but it also brings you the guide book that is indispensable to attainment of victory at the shows. As you become a member of your breed club, and as you become more proficient as a breeder of your chosen breed, you may serve to improve your club's guide book.

I will describe one excellent guide book to give you an idea of what you might expect—the **Guide Book of the American Dutch Rabbit Club.**

It contains eighty-eight pages and is printed professionally, with type, photography, and other illustrations of high quality, surrounded by a two-color cover. It contains a history of the breed, the standard, just as it is in the ARBA **Standard of Perfection**; superb line drawings of the all-important markings and other specifications, a wide variety of articles on breeding tips by expert breeders, a listing of the names of breeders who have won the ARBA national convention show over the years, and even advertisements of breeders who are members and who have stock for sale.

Anyone who expects to start out with Dutch and be a success at the show table must study, in particular, the articles by experts and the drawings in addition to the standard itself, which this additional information, in effect, interprets. Quite helpful is the special glossary of terms that apply specifically to this breed. You have to learn the jargon of the breed in order to discuss the breed intelligently or even to get the most out of the articles.

Health, Vitality, Production

Many breed guide books are lacking in advice about breeding goals **other** than conformation to the standard **appearance** of the specimen. Before you can even consider type, markings, color, etc., you must make sure you are putting all the appearance factors on healthy, productive stock. Appearance must be secondary.

Of course, it all goes back to your original stock. You selected a breeder from whom to buy on the basis of his winnings, because he kept his breeding stock registered—in other words because his rabbits consistently conformed to the standard specifications for **appearance**. But in addition you must have considered the productivity of his stock, which has a lot to do with health and vitality.

If the breeder who sold you your foundation stock was one who bred his rabbits all year round, and if you do so also, you will not only produce a great number of rabbits from which to select your show entries and future breeders, you will have avoided some problems. You want does that are productive and bucks that are eager to serve them. The best way I know to assure productivity is to select breeding stock that is among your most productive and to keep it producing.

Save youngsters from large litters and soon you will increase litter size. This is particularly important in the smaller breeds, where you naturally get smaller litters, but it is also significant in the medium breeds, some of which will not produce eight or so on a regular basis unless bred specifically to do so. And while I'll soon get into feeding youngsters, there is no reason why, with today's feeds and proper feeding programs, your fancy does can't raise litters the way commercial does do. It's a reasonable goal you should be shooting for.

Three Keys to Success In Breeding

To build a herd of consistent winners, breed with three points in mind:

1. Selection of sire and dam to mate is uppermost in importance.

2. Linebreeding (a form of inbreeding) is your second avenue to success.

3. Constant breeding, all year round, to insure productivity and **to produce as many new generations as possible** will help you get ahead of the competition.

First, let's look at selection. This is a process that begins the day the rabbits are born, continues until you mate them, and often is revised one or more times after their first offspring are born and have matured.

On the day of kindling you will want to cull (the opposite of select) any dead, deformed, or runty youngsters. If you are raising a marked breed, you will be able to cull any mismarked young as well, if you want to.

You should breed two or more does on the same day so that you will be able to foster youngsters to other litters to even up litter size. If one doe has a small litter and another one has a great number, give the former one some extra youngsters to bring up.

If the litter is too large for the doe to raise and you have no other doe to receive some young, you must dispose of those youngsters to best advantage—removing those that are uneven in size or are mismarked. If you have been selecting good productive does that have a good milk supply, you should expect them to raise litters of eight. The notion that you should reduce the litter size to give the youngsters more milk and a better start simply does not stand up with today's delicately balanced pelleted feeds, protein supplements, milk replacers, creep feed, special feeders, and professional feeding programs specified by feed companies. So look forward to producing large healthy litters of the healthiest **and** best looking young.

Records Are Essential

Keep hutch record cards to preserve kindling and pedigree information. Don't try to do this in your head, because even in a very small rabbitry there will be too much to remember, no matter how good your memory is. Mark down the litter size and any bits of information, such as the number born dead, deformed, mismarked, off-color, runty, etc., etc. Indicate where the fostered babies went. Of course, record the name or number of the sire.

Selection continues at weaning time, although you have been looking the youngsters over each day since they were born. Type is somewhat obscured by baby fur, but it's safe to say that hindquarters probably won't ever get any better than they are the day the babies are born, although shoulders probably will. The key to selection, of course, is your standard. I can't tell you **specifically** what to look for without knowing your breed, but your **Standard of Perfection** certainly can, and so can your breed guide book. You should familiarize yourself with both so that you can make judgments about growing youngsters, judgments that you may have to live with after weaning time. Because it's at weaning time, ordinarily, when you give each youngster its own hutch, that you must select the keepers.

Young Florida White buck.

Small Breeds Offer Advantages

Selection at weaning time is as much a function of hutch space as almost anything else, but there is something additional to consider. If you have several really good ones and can't make up your mind just yet which ones to keep, you do have an advantage with smaller breeds. They require smaller hutches, which lets you keep more rabbits in a given space. And two can usually eat for the price of one—the smaller rabbits hold down the feed bill. Also, larger rabbits that eventually are to be culled may not bring you the fryer meat price from some processors because they get too large—usually over 6 pounds. But the smaller breeds will bring you that price, or even sell as little pets, for a much greater period, perhaps their entire lives.

Selection at this point has a two-fold aim. The first part is showing the animal as a junior: the second is breeding it as a senior.

Naturally, you want to select your young for the shows with the standard in mind. And you want each young rabbit to come as close to that standard as possible.

Looking Ahead

Each rabbit I keep I consider as one-half of a breeding team. I don't view the rabbit as a rabbit in itself, but as one-half of what will produce the next generation. It's a little game of dissatisfaction in a way. I never really settle for what I have. I view it only as a means to something even better.

Therefore, I keep the rabbit because I feel it will approach the standard very closely, but also because it will mate well with another I have selected.

The Perfect Rabbit

No single rabbit has it all, and never will, and it's a good thing. Every once in a while you will hear some novice announce that he has bred the "perfect" Dutch or English Spot or whatever, and you have to chuckle. Because not only is he obviously unfamiliar with the standard, you know that should a rabbit come too close to matching the standard, the committee would revise the standard to make it more difficult to attain. Nobody has yet bred the "perfect" rabbit and nobody ever will, not as long as we have a vigilant standards committee. Besides, who in the world would really want to breed the "perfect" rabbit? I mean, where would we go from there?

So when I say each animal is only one-half of the next breeding team, I mean that I am looking for complementary attributes—qualities in one animal that I can apply to an animal with different qualities, to the benefit of the subsequent offspring. These are evident to me because of my knowledge of the bloodlines I'm working with in addition to the appearance of the specific animals.

In practice, most successful breeders maintain several bloodlines with the strain that they have or are trying to conceive. To illustrate this, take a look at my Tans. I have one "line" with very sharp markings and very "even" undercolor, which is desirable in Tans. Another line has richer undercolor and better type. Still another has better fur quality, and another has emerged as most productive. I am constantly mixing these features like an artist mixing colors on his palette, but I am maintaining the identity of each line, too. The way I do all this is by inbreeding on a line, or linebreeding.

The Practice of Linebreeding

Linebreeding is a form of inbreeding, which is, of course, the breeding of close relatives. But mere inbreeding without linebreeding won't necessarily improve your stock over the long run. The major goal, of course, is to slowly but surely improve the stock, all the while winning **consistently** year after year. I should add that outcrossing, or going outside the bloodlines that you are working with, might give you a winner this year, and, in fact, may certainly improve your stock so it wins consistently in the future as, perhaps, it might not have in the past. And I don't mean to suggest that a judicious outcross isn't occasionally the wise course to take. But to maintain an orderly progression toward overall improvement, it is wise to stay within the bloodlines one has as much as possible, and to do it on a line.

The line of progression is maintained by mating offspring back to parents and grandparents, uncles, aunts, great uncles, great aunts, and even older ancestors, as long as those forebears have something to offer the succeeding generation.

Let's take a look at a good buck. He's a grand champion. He has sired many litters. He has children, grandchildren, and great-grandchildren. He has them because he is that one excellent buck that comes along every now and then and outshines his contemporaries. And he keeps getting the opportunity to sire more young as long as none of his issue is superior to him. Obviously, the overall goal of any breeding pair is to produce young equal to or better than their parents. And when a better young buck comes along, perhaps one with all his predecessor's qualities (and a proven ability to pass these qualities along), but, let's say, with better color, the old buck must retire.

The younger buck becomes next in the line of succession of sires, therefore, and contributes to general improvement of the bloodline in this scheme called linebreeding.

Children Prove the Parents

How do we know this young buck is better (or even any good at all)? Mere **selection** isn't sufficient to make this judgment. We have selected this buck, but the only way to determine his worth as a sire is to examine his children. The children, as they say, **prove** the parents. Are the children of this buck even better than those of the old buck? By better, I mean do they come even closer in appearance to the standard? Are they healthy and productive? Only when such is the case, and consistently, with a number of different dams in your herd, can you consider replacing the old buck in this linebreeding progression.

Of course, this is of the utmost importance. One selects breeding pairs and maintains and improves the line, but only when the succeeding youngsters prove that this is wise. One certainly does not breed on the line for the sake of a line. Several rabbit publications contain linebreeding charts, and some breeders have attempted to duplicate them simply for the sake of the chart and to produce bloodlines and sub-bloodlines in accordance with the chart. Of course, this is ridiculous. Selection and performance of the offspring are the determinants, and nothing else. The charts merely show the percentage of "blood" that sires and dams pass along in succeeding generations if certain matings are made, and you may draw some conclusions from this. But charts don't dictate these matings.

Production Is Important

Once you have established your breeding program by choosing which sires and dams you will use and which characteristics you will attempt to "fix" in your succeeding generations, you are left with still another way to succeed. You must remember that your competitors are doing the same thing. They, too, are selecting their best young stock as replacements for the older generations. If your stock and theirs are of about the same quality, you are on even footing now and you are pitting your abilities at selection and linebreeding against theirs.

But suppose they breed for only one or two litters per year per doe? And suppose you are breeding four to six litters per year per doe? You are going to work harder at it, have more rabbits to select from (and more to sell one way or another—or eat), and you are going to be able to outpace the competition.

Constant breeding is thus the third important key to success. The more you breed and the more youngsters you get, the more stock you have to select from, to be sure, but also the faster more of them will reach maturity. You will get from one generation to the next sooner than your competitors. You will write a lot of pedigrees and you will replace more of that old stock in your line a lot sooner than will the other guy. And if you are staying close to the standard for appearance, watching for health and vitality, choosing also for productivity and letting the **children prove the parents**, you will come out ahead in the race for overall improvement that will make you the winner.

You might read books on genetics. You might draw elaborate charts, but I don't think that's necessary. You certainly must keep pedigree and other breeding records. But if you study the **Standard of Perfection** and your breed guide book, start with top-notch stock, select your future breeders carefully, and settle on them only after their children have **proved** you were correct, and then outproduce your competition to get yourself to the next generation and the whole process all over again just a bit faster, you will be a winner at the rabbit shows.

Planning for Winners

When the day of the big show arrives, do you simply enter the stock that looks good to you and hope the judge agrees? Not if you wish to be a consistent winner. You must have done some planning. And you must have started it months in advance, with one eye on the calendar.

Of course, if you attend several shows each spring and fall, as do many exhibitors, you may not be concerned with the specific date of a certain show, but you should at least keep the general period of time in mind.

Let's examine some ways that planning with the calendar can help make you a winner. One of these is to attempt to enter stock that is at the best age to win. Juniors should be almost 6 months old, which is the top of their age limit and, if possible, into their first adult coats, which usually occurs at 5-6 months. Exactly what this age will be is something you will have to determine by experience. Seniors should be in their first year or 18 months—no older in most cases, to make sure they have the firm flesh, good color, and full bloom of youthful maturity.

You don't want your juniors so young they are outclassed in size and weight and fur condition, and you don't want your seniors to be over the hill. So keep an eye on the calendar, know what you are shooting for and then breed your rabbits accordingly to give you entries that are most likely to win. Of course, this can work another way, too. Many breeders find that the best body type and ear length occur in rabbits born in late fall and winter.

Don't expect to win much with a doe that has had a litter. First of all, she pulls out a lot of fur to make a nest, and it doesn't always grow back with the best coloring. Second, it's nearly impossible to get her back into top flesh condition. The big question that often arises is whether to breed the doe when first she is ready or to save her for an upcoming show.

Keep the Does at Home
The answer is often a personal one, something you must decide for yourself. In my situation, I practically never save a doe for a show. I have found that if you don't breed some does when first they are ready you will never get them bred, because they develop internal fat that stops their eggs from descending the fallopian tubes to be fertilized. I like to breed my Tan does at five months, even if a great show is only a couple of months away. For this reason I rarely show many senior does, and, in fact, in 20 years of showing, I have produced only four grand champion does that I have exhibited myself.

A grand champion must have at least one qualifying win as a senior, and I find that one difficult to attain in the case of a doe. In my last such attempt I had a beautiful Black Tan doe that won Best of Breed in two successive shows only weeks apart. As she neared six months of age and was ready to breed, the last spring show of the season was only a week away. I confidently mated her before the show but she came in only second in her class of nine. By the following fall, she had raised the litter but was in no shape to show and she wasn't shown again. Her litter contained a nice little buck that I showed as a junior in the ARBA Convention Show in October. He won Best of Breed. Had I held her back for showing in the fall I never would have won in October. And this young buck soon became a grand champion himself. Thus I am able to rationalize the whole procedure.

Avoiding a Nip Here and There

The doe often even suffers some disfigurement during mating, because the buck enjoys taking a nip of fur out of her shoulders. If you have a doe that you want to mate before a show, restrain her for mating and hold a piece of burlap or canvas over her shoulders. Let the buck bite that instead.

It's not just the does who lose fur in the mating process, however. Sometimes the doe will nip the buck a good one. Again, restraining the doe for mating often saves wear and tear on the pelt of a buck you plan to show.

Time for the Checkup

At weaning time, when you select young stock to show and keep for future breeding, it's a good idea to record each rabbit's ear number, sire and dam, and date of birth in a stock record book, along with any comments that might occur to you as you examine each individual. Certainly you will want to check for any disqualifications, such as white spots or off-colored toenails or eyes.

It's amazing how many disqualified rabbits appear on show tables simply because their owners never took the time to give them the once-over at weaning time. It's all the more unfortunate when you think of all the time they have been feeding the rabbit when it should have been feeding them. And consider that it took up valuable hutch space that should have been reserved for a littermate. Not to mention a wasted entry fee.

You must give each buck his own hutch at weaning time. You can keep young does together for a while, but be on the alert for fur-chewing. If one chews the fur off another, it will take time to grow back before you can expect to win anything with it.

Not only do I attempt to give each doe its own hutch at weaning time, I also make sure that my bucks go in my lower tier of hutches, and that they get solid hutch partitions if they tend to be urine sprayers. I don't need any urine sprayed on the coats of stock I plan to show.

The Right Light, The Right Hutch

Because my rabbits are of four different colors, I'm especially careful to make certain that direct sunlight does not fall on them. With white rabbits, sunlight, and its bleaching capability, is not a bad idea if it doesn't overheat them.

While each rabbit needs its own hutch, it also needs one of sufficient size. Developing young stock need enough room to exercise. It is a mistake to cram them into tiny holding pens, and you will learn this if a judge tells you your young rabbits are not in firm flesh condition, or that they have a fatty roll over the shoulders. One way to make sure the rabbits develop properly is to put a wooden box into the hutch. The rabbit will jump up onto it and down several times a day, putting more muscle on the shoulders.

Pellets—The Foundation Diet

As the show date approaches, the way your rabbits are fed will affect flesh and fur condition more than anything else. Of course, correct feeding is something that begins as soon as the youngsters hop out of the nest box. A good start includes a complete pellet as a mainstay, but you can add creep feed, rolled or crimped oats, bread and milk and Calf Manna to the diet of the pre-weaners and their dam. They should get all the feed they can consume.

Once weaned, you will want to put them on a ration of pellets, perhaps supplemented with hay and oats, giving them all they will clean up in the period between feedings, which may be every 12 hours or every 24. I feed once a day, in the evening. Regular feeding times are important. Many good stockmen feed their animals in the evening before they sit down to their own meal.

When your youngsters are 2–4 months old, you shouldn't mess around with their diets. Pellets, oats, hay—that's about it. You must be careful with rabbits of this age. Not only do you want them to grow properly with all the nutritional elements they require, but you have to watch out for diarrhea. Young rabbits are very susceptible to diarrhea, and if they get it you can just about forget showing them, depending on how young they are and how severe a case they get. Once they get that pinched and chopped look around the hindquarters, don't plan on them ever winning anything, or being worth keeping as breeders. To avoid this, be extra careful about their diets at this age. In addition, it is wise to medicate their feed or water regularly and during times of stress. Several rabbitry supply firms have medications available. I recommend Neo-Terramycin.

As young rabbits reach their mature weight you will want to limit their feed, according to size and weight. It varies greatly from breed to breed. Several weeks before an upcoming show you may want to increase their feed, or utilize feeds or supplements that will improve their condition.

Change Gradually

There are quite a few special conditioning feeding techniques, but behind them all is the fact that you must change to the conditioning feed gradually, and that you must only gradually increase the amount you give. Here are some feeds and supplements used by successful exhibitors: dry dog food; coarse, sweet, mixed horse feed; oats; sunflower seeds; mangel beets; Calf Manna; wheat germ oil.

You have to be careful using these feeds. Don't overdo it. Keep rabbits on pellets and hay, and add a little of one or more of these feeds, increasing the amounts gradually each day. The dog food and the horse feed, the sunflower seeds and the wheat germ oil (poured right on the pellets) seem to do the most for fur condition. Oats, Calf Manna, and mangel beets add to flesh condition. You have to consider ideal and top weight limits. Work gradually toward the weight you want to reach. If you get there too soon, and find you have to cut back the feed, the result will be flabbiness and no trophy. Once you attain top fur condition, go easy on the oil and oil seeds to avoid having the coat break into a moult.

One feed to avoid is greens. Greens will not build good hard flesh, and they are likely to cause diarrhea, which can set the rabbit back or even ruin it.

Water Keeps Them Eating

The cheapest feed is water. Rabbits must have a constant supply to keep them eating properly. And it must be fresh and inviting. Consider installing an automatic watering system, which is the best way to deliver fresh water. And it's easier on

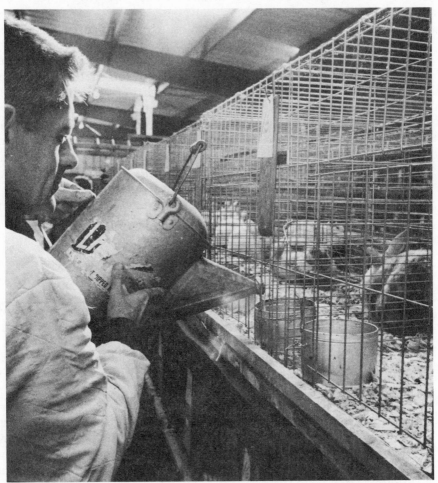

Watering rabbits at a show.

you, too. Most of the work in rabbits is hand watering. You will have more time to work with your rabbits in more productive ways if you aren't spending a lot of time watering.

So far you have selected the young rabbits to show, and you are feeding them with the show date in mind. What else can you do to help yourself?

Keep the rabbit's nails trimmed with wire cutters or toenail clippers. If the nails are too long and he pulls one out on the wire floor, he's disqualified.

Pick him up correctly. Put one hand under his chest and the other under his rump. Don't grab him by the skin over the shoulders—it will only loosen it, and, besides, you might yank out some fur.

Teach him to pose. Place him on a piece of carpet or burlap sack on a solid base and pose him correctly, in accordance with his type and breed. You might use a soft bristle brush on him at this time—or even a slicker brush (with curved metal tines) if his fur has any mats. If you handle him correctly and confidently and teach him to pose for just a minute or two each day for weeks before the show, you stand a better chance. First, he will show off his attributes much better. And, of course, he's not likely to win the judge's nod if he's a scratcher or a biter or if he leaps all over the table. These are the little things that can make a big difference and they are important when the competition gets stiff. You have to help yourself in every way to be a winner.

Learning About Shows

While nearly 1,000 rabbit shows take place each year in the United States, you probably never have read about one in your local newspaper. As a participant activity, rather than a spectator sport, it's rare that rabbit shows get publicity except in rabbit publications. So that's where you should look to find out when and where you'll find them.

Shows generally take place in the spring and fall. Summer's really too hot in most sections of the country, and travel is uncertain in the winter in many areas.

To find out everything you need to know about an upcoming show, read the show catalog. To obtain it, watch for listings of shows by date and name, along with the address of the show secretary, in each issue of **Domestic Rabbits** magazine, in the newsletters of the national breed clubs, and in those of local clubs and state associations.

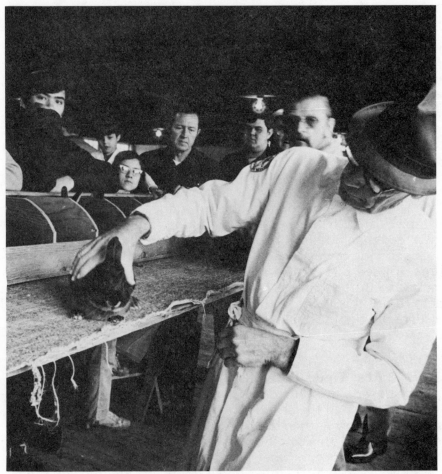

Exhibitors watch judge look over a Tan.

When you find a show listed at a time and place that are convenient, write to the show secretary and request the free catalog. This is a publication that will not arrive by return mail but, rather, when the catalog chairman gets it mimeographed or printed. He chooses a date that gives you enough time to plan, but one that allows him to put the catalog together, including all the prizes and specials, some of which may come in at the last minute. Once you attend a show you usually get on the mailing list to receive the catalog for the next show of the club without making a special request. But it's still a good idea to keep an eye on **Domestic Rabbits** and other listings.

Look For Sanction

When you get the catalog, look for several items. First, make sure your breed is sanctioned. The catalog will list breeds for which there are sweepstakes or sanctions. Both terms mean the same thing—that you can win points toward the sweepstakes awards in your breed club, provided, of course, that you are a member. Usually, there are more shows in a locale than you reasonably can expect to attend in a year. So it's a good idea, when possible, to choose the shows at which your breed is sanctioned. Some state and regional associations also have sweepstakes. If you are a member, you may want to enter only those shows sanctioned by the association.

The catalog will include a list of judges. I usually look this list over carefully, because certain judges are better at judging my breed than others. If I don't see the name of a judge I feel will do a good job on my breed, I may pass up the show. At the same time, if I see one I know to be better than average, I not only make an effort to attend, I try to persuade the show superintendent to put this judge on my breed. The show superintendents reserve the right to make judging assignments, but they aim to please.

Check Dates, Times Carefully

Look for a deadline date for mailing entries and a deadline hour for arrival in the showroom on the day of the show. Some shows will allow entries the day of the show and some will not. You must read the catalog very carefully to avoid the disappointment that occurs when you think they will take entries on the show day, drive 100 miles to get there, and are told you can't enter your rabbits.

An entry blank is included. You must fill this out and return it to the show secretary. Exactly how you do this can make a big difference in whether you are a winner or a loser. There are a great many things to consider when making out this entry blank.

One is cost. It costs $1.25 to $1.50 or more these days to enter a rabbit in the open or regular class. Fur entries usually are another 50 cents or a dollar. At fair shows the price may be lower.

So you have twenty-five or fifty rabbits that you think are potential winners, but can you afford to enter that many? At some fair shows, where there is a lot of prize money, it really pays off to enter that many rabbits or more, because premiums are paid right down to fifth place. But at most local shows it is to your advantage to select more carefully those rabbits you will enter.

Several Considerations

After you look at the cost of entering, consider the entry blank in other ways. There are a certain number of classes available to enter in each breed, depending upon the size of the breed and the number of varieties in it. Medium and giant breeds have junior, 6- to 8-month and senior classes in each variety. The smaller breeds have only junior and senior classes in each variety.

Consider the entry blank in terms of prizes offered. For example, if there is a trophy offered for best junior, you might want to include a junior even though you have a senior you think is better.

Are you after sweepstakes points in a big way? You may want to put as many as five rabbits in each class, because sweepstakes points are awarded down to fifth.

Do you want to improve your chances of winning a grand championship leg in a breed that normally has a small entry? Perhaps you should enter at least three animals in a single class. If two other breeders each enter one in the same class, one of the three of you is going to win a grand championship leg, because there must be at least five rabbits and three exhibitors for a leg to be awarded to a class winner. And don't be bashful about sharing entry information with fellow breeders. Let your competitors know what you plan to enter if you think there may be trouble mustering enough entries in a class to win a leg. Encourage them to enter stock in that class.

Do you want to make the greatest possible effort to win Best of Variety? Make sure you enter juniors and seniors (and 6–8s if in the larger breeds) of both sexes, because class winners stay on the table for judging of Best of Breed and Best Opposite Sex. The more classes you enter, the more you are likely to win and the better your chance to take the top two awards.

You do realize, of course, that only one rabbit wins best and one best opposite in a single breed. Could you take only two rabbits and win it all? Recently a young lady from Utah, traveled to a show in Colorado and won Best in Show, over hundreds of rabbits, with the only representative of this breed that was entered that day. Not just entered by her, but the only member of the breed entered by anyone. And that's not the first time this has happened.

Can You Beat Yourself?

Should you enter your best rabbit every time? If you do, you might beat yourself. Suppose you entered two rabbits in the same class, and they finished one-two, but the one that came in second needed only one more leg to make it a grand champion. Should you have entered the winner even though it now has a leg? You may never get the third leg on the other rabbit.

Should you enter a grand champion? If it wins you beat not only the competition, but again, you also beat yourself. And for what? A grand champion is still only a grand champion after it wins three legs. But now it has prevented another rabbit from winning the same honor. If it's a very important show, and you need the sweepstakes points, or there is a big prize to be won, you may want to enter a grand champion, but ordinarily, most breeders don't. It is a controversial question, and one that you must decide for yourself on an individual show basis. Three legs makes a grand champion. Four or more is gilding the lily.

So we have many considerations here, including the fact that you may not even want to enter the best rabbit you have. But let's look at the entry blank from probably the most important standpoint—what do I have that is likely to win?

Judge Your Own Stock

A junior rabbit just under 6 months old probably will beat a 12-week junior, all else being equal. A 6–8 rabbit just under 8 months probably will beat a 6-month rabbit, all else being equal. And a senior rabbit in its first year or 18 months probably will beat an older senior, which may have become flabby with age or have lost some of its sparkling color. Choosing a rabbit at the top of its class in age and weight for juniors and 6–8s, and in its prime for seniors, will go a long way toward choosing a winner.

Prime flesh and fur condition also are important. There is very little percentage in entering an animal that is out of condition—thin, flabby, moulting, or hutch-stained. You should have been working for weeks before the show to achieve the peak of condition, but sometimes, despite your best efforts, it either eludes you or peaks too soon and fades away. When you are making out that entry blank, look for top condition.

What you are doing is prejudging your stock. But if you have entries in all the right classes, by sex, age, and variety, and you really can't narrow down the choice as much as you like, take more rabbits. You may have one rabbit with better type and another with better color—so why not let the judge choose? You will get the benefit of his comments on all of the rabbits you enter, you may cop all the top places, and your betting favorite might not be the one the judge likes best. Sometimes it's a good idea to take more rabbits than you really want to take.

A related suggestion when making out the entry blank is in order: don't get to the show, look over the competition, and wish you had brought something you left home. Many times I hear a breeder say he wishes he had brought a certain rabbit because he thinks it is better than some he sees on the judge's table. It may be wishful thinking. It may be sour grapes. Or he may be right! If you aren't sure about whether to enter a certain animal, perhaps because it is slightly out of condition, enter it anyway. For $1.50 you will get rid of the nagging doubt.

How I Fill Out the Entry Blank

To get right down to the reality of the situation, let's take a look at an entry blank I have before me and discuss how I'll fill it out. It's for the first show of the season, two weeks away. Let's see if I can help myself to the trophy.

I'm raising Tans, which have only junior and senior classes, and which have four varieties, Black, Blue, Chocolate, and Lilac. The show is sanctioned by the Tan Club, which means I certainly want to attend and win as many sweepstakes points as I can. There is a trophy for Best of Breed and a plaque for Best Opposite Sex. There are rosettes and money on the best and best opposite of each variety, and a couple of other prizes.

First I look at the Blacks. I have a very nice little junior buck that will be about 5 months old. I'll put him in. I have two junior does, sisters, about the same age as the buck. I'll put in one that I think is better looking, and mate the other. I don't have a senior doe to enter, because all are either expecting or nursing litters. I don't have a senior buck to enter. I have only two at present, and both are grand champions, so I won't enter either one. So I enter a junior buck and a junior doe.

Raising Hopes for a 'Leg'

In Blues, I have two senior bucks. Each has two legs on a grand championship. One is a couple of years old and hasn't won much lately but has sired a convention Best of Breed winner. The other was Best Opposite Blue at last fall's national convention, the last time he was shown.

I'll put them both in, even though the younger one is better. The older buck **might** win, making him a grand champion after all, although I've really given up on that. Also, by entering two in the class, one that usually has a small entry, I'm increasing the chance that **somebody** will win a grand championship leg, even if it isn't me. But I hope it's me. And I hope it's on the older buck, because the younger one will pick his up some time later. I'm willing to bet on that.

I have three blue junior bucks. One is about 5 months and is my betting favorite. In fact, he's better than either of the two senior blue bucks, in my opinion. The other two are littermates, about 3½ months old. I'll enter them both, which puts three in the class. If two other breeders each enter at least one blue junior buck, there will be a leg to win in that class.

In blue does, again, no senior. They are all too busy. In juniors, I have one about 5 months and one about 3½ months. I'll enter them both, for the same reason that I entered all I had to enter in the other blue classes. There aren't that many Blues around so the classes need all the help I can give them.

So far I've entered two Blacks and seven Blues. I do have some other Blacks and Blues—old does, the two grand champions I mentioned, and some youngsters that were born only in December, and which I think would be outclassed by the others. They will get a chance to go to the shows later in the spring.

What I Really Want To Win

Now to the Chocolates. I have one grand champion buck. He stays home. I have a very nice young senior, born last summer. He has been shown twice. He went Best of Breed in his first time out and then was the first junior chocolate buck at the ARBA Convention show. So he's got two grand championship legs. I'm betting that he will go Best Chocolate at this show and become a grand champion. I have four other nice chocolate senior bucks which have never been shown. They were born late last summer, but I had so many good young chocolate juniors that were a little older that they never got to any of the shows. And I'm not taking them to this one either, because if one should knock off the buck that has two legs already, I'd really be upset. Unless I miss my guess, there will be plenty of Chocolates there, so there's no need to load up the classes. I want to make a grand champion out of the buck that has two legs. I already know he's a good breeder, as he has sired several fine litters. He's out of a pair of grand champions, a rare Tan couple, and he looks like he will be the next successor to my current grand champion chocolate buck, born two years ago. So I'm betting on this guy to get that third leg. In fact, this is what I really want out of the whole show, if you come right down to it.

I have three nice junior bucks, littermates, 5 months old. They go. I have a chocolate senior doe. I shouldn't have, but I do. I have a very nice doe that was supposed to have a litter this week—it would have been her first. But she missed. I've got to mate her back, but I'll just wait a week, so she will only be a week along on the show date. She's in fine condition—perhaps too fine to have a litter. By that I mean she may be a little heavy for breeding, but she looks terrific for show. It's not the way I planned it, but let's face reality, there she is. So she'll go to the show.

I Might Sell One First

In junior chocolate does, I have three that are old enough—one's about 5 months and two are about 4 months. The one that is 5 months is just about ready to be bred, but I'll hold off a couple of weeks so she can make this show. It will be her first and only if everything works out. I'll mate her after the show, and she'll be raising babies this spring instead of winning ribbons. I'm going to enter the other two junior does—unless I sell one of them first. Somebody's coming over to take a look at her. If he puts the money in my hand I'll have only two junior chocolate does to enter instead of three.

Now my entry is up to seventeen. Because I usually enter about twenty or so, I'm getting about up to my average. And I still have to enter something in Lilacs.

I have no lilac senior bucks to enter. I have one grand champion who stays home. I have a lilac senior doe, which missed on her first turn. The day she was due was bitter cold, so it's probably just as well. I keep telling myself that. Anyway, I'm going to enter her.

One litter born in November, 4 months ago, produced two excellent little does and a buck. One of the does is the best of the three. I'll enter both does and the buck. If I had more Lilacs I'd probably enter them, too. Actually, I do have some that are only about 10 weeks old—3 months by the show date, but I'll let them stay because I just know that these older ones would beat them.

The Best Percentage Is Mine

This gives me twenty-one rabbits to enter. And it really was easy, at this time of year, to select them from the 100 or so rabbits that I keep. Because at this time of year, especially coming off a very cold December and January, fur is in great condition. No moulting. And the rabbits really have been eating well, what with all the cold weather. The key to keeping them eating well in cold weather, of course, is to provide plenty of warm water for drinking.

So with twenty-one entries, I have twenty-one chances to win Best of Breed. All my entries are in one breed, with the four varieties.

A few exhibitors will enter more than I will, but I'm betting most of them will enter more than one breed. In terms of sheer numbers, I have given myself the best percentage of a chance to win in my breed. I'm guessing that because this is the first show of the season, with lots of exhibitors eager to get to the show, the number of Tans will approach 100, which is a nice bunch of Tans, and probably the biggest entry until the All-Tan or the ARBA Convention Show. We have had more than that at our area shows, but only on a few occasions.

Nevertheless, 20 percent of them will be mine. There probably will be about eight or nine other exhibitors of Tans, perhaps a dozen. But one of every five rabbits on the table will be mine. I have a very good opportunity to take home the top trophy. And you can see that if I do, it won't be by accident. I'm doing everything I can to tip the scales in my favor. Not just to beat the other exhibitors, but to have **certain** rabbits win. The ones that need grand championship legs when possible.

Twelve Shots at the Trophy

I'll have something in almost every class—twelve of the sixteen. That gives me a dozen chances to put something in the finals for Best of Breed. Some of my competitors do not raise all four colors, so I have an advantage in that I have four varieties in which to compete for Best of Breed. If I were to make the maximum effort—sixteen classes—I would improve my chances more. But then I'd miss out on those extra litters the senior does who stay home are having. I'd miss my chance to get into the next generation ahead of my competitors. I want to breed into the next generation so I can improve my stock overall faster than they do. That's how I got twenty-one nice Tans to enter here today in the first place. If I had taken my senior does to the shows last fall, these juniors wouldn't be here today, and whatever was here probably wouldn't look as good as it does. To me anyway. And the judge, I hope.

I have twenty-one rabbits entered in the regular or open classes. Let's take a look at the fur class. It's a funny thing with Tans. They go in normal colored fur. But, actually, their fur has more sheen than that of a Satin, which isn't allowed in normal colored fur. When you get a fur judge who is impressed by sheen, Tans are the big winners. Their density, however, often is not all that it is on some breeds, and when you have a judge who is swayed by density, you lose. I have had my Tans take the top places and the bottom places in the fur class, but never in the middle.

Two For a Dollar

At most shows the entry fee is 50 cents and first prize is 50 percent of the entry fees of all those entered. If twenty-five were entered in normal colored fur, first place could win $6.25. There are smaller percentages for lower places. But in this show they are offering only a rosette, so I'm tempted to say the heck with it. On the other hand, maybe I'll just look over some of that chocolate and black fur on these regular class entries and put two (for a dollar) in the normal colored fur class.

The entry blank is a carbon paper set, and you are supposed to send in all copies, as they are used in the show report you get later. What I do, however, is make an additional carbon copy for my own record. I don't want to send in my entry and then forget which rabbits I'm supposed to take. I'll need the carbon copy when I load up my carriers on the day of the show.

I Send No Money

I put my entry blank in the mail **without** the entry fee unless it is specifically required. Some shows will not refund your money if you cannot attend, or if you scratch certain rabbits that you may at the last minute have decided not to enter for one reason or another. I prefer to pay the entry fees upon arrival.

By joining me as I pondered filling out this entry blank, you can see that it is a procedure you should calculate very carefully. You want to make every move to help yourself win—over the competition and what you want most.

If you have mailed in your entry blank, you won't have to leave as early on the day of the show as you will if you are going to enter them on this day. Entries usually close early in the morning, but rabbits don't have to be in the showroom until nearly noon at most shows. At one upcoming show, for example, the catalog states that entries close at 10 a.m. but rabbits don't have to be in the showroom until 11:30. Generally speaking, rabbit shows don't start on time. That is, the judging doesn't start on time; but the rabbits have to be there at the deadline hour. If they aren't there, judging is delayed or the late arrivals are simply left out.

What To Take With You

Since traffic usually is light early on Sunday mornings, you should have a quick trip, but allow more than enough time. And don't leave without taking a few things you will need: a black felt-tip marker, a roll of masking tape, a grooming brush, the show catalog, and, perhaps, a road map.

And don't forget the rabbits. But before you put the rabbits in the car, check each one carefully against the carbon copy of your entry blank to make sure you're taking along the right ones. Check its permanent tattooed ear number for accuracy and legibility. Also, check to make sure it's the sex you thought it was, and that it has no cold or sore hocks or anything else that would cause it to be **eliminated.** Rabbits are eliminated for various **temporary** problems. Entering it in the wrong class because of sex will cause it to be eliminated. Then check for **disqualifications.** These are permanent defects and include malloclusion (bad teeth), off-color toenails, white or colored spots where they don't belong, missing testicles, blindness, and others. Both eliminations and disqualifications are listed and described in the **Standard of Perfection.** That's something else you ought to take along with you.

Should you encounter a rabbit with such a problem, you may substitute another rabbit in the same class—that is, the same age, variety, and sex—provided you notify the show secretary and have the entry records changed at the show.

The All-Wire Carrier

When you have located all the right rabbits and they all pass your final inspection, load them into their carriers. Carriers for rabbits may be merely wire-bound vegetable crates bedded with shavings, or you may want to use wire carriers, with wire floors and pans underneath. That's what I recommend. A solid floor with shavings is not ideal for travel because the rabbit may be stained and overheated, both of which affect its condition. Of course, if the rabbit becomes too hot, it may die.

All-wire carriers, like all-wire hutches, allow plenty of fresh air and keep the rabbits clean. If you put your rabbits in the trunk of your car, with the lid cracked open and tied down, they will travel nicely in wire carriers. Do not put dishes of water in the carriers, as they will only spill and mat the rabbits' fur. Use water bottles if you will be making a long trip. A couple of handfuls of alfalfa hay make good eating along the way, but you can include pellets if the trip is very long. If your rabbits are used to a piece of carrot and apple, put them in the carrier. Do not put them in, however, if you think they may cause diarrhea, which not only is bad in itself, but can cause the rabbit to be eliminated by the judge.

Don't let direct sunlight shine on your rabbits in the car. Put a feed sack or the Sunday newspaper over the top of the carrier for shade. Sometimes it gets hotter under a large car rear window than you realize.

Where To Go

Upon arrival, leave the rabbits in the car and go directly to the show secretary's table, taking your entry blank with you. Pay your entry fee and pick up your show cards, of which there usually are two for each rabbit entered.

One card has the rabbit's show number on it. If this is a "carrying cage show," tape this card to the carrier with a piece across the top and one across the bottom. Make sure you have

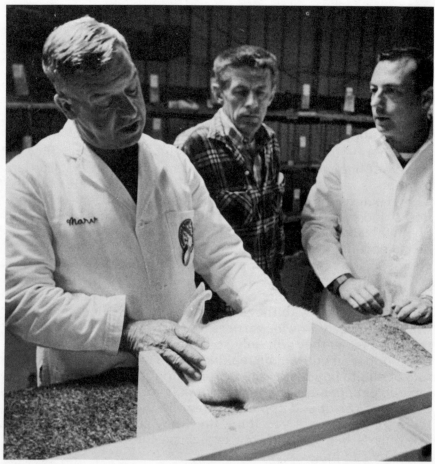

Judging New Zealand Whites.

the matching show number or "coop number" card that has space allocated for judge's remarks, and slip it under the first card. Write the "coop number" or show number in the rabbit's **right** ear with your felt-tip marker. Remember, the left one has its permanent tattoo number in it. Give the rabbit a last-minute check and possibly the once-over-lightly with the grooming brush.

When all the rabbits are ear-marked and all the carriers have the cards in place, take the rabbits into the showroom, where you will find carriers lined up in the numerical sequence of coop numbers. Place your carriers in their proper position.

If this is a cooped show, you will find numbered coops and you transfer your rabbits to the coops, stowing your carriers under the coops or back in the car.

Handle With Care

Be especially careful about how you handle your stock. Place one hand under the rabbit's chest and the other one under its hindquarters. Tuck its head into the crook of your elbow and carry it like a football—or the way a football is supposed to be carried.

Don't grab the rabbit by the scruff of the neck. You will pull out fur, loosen flesh over the shoulders, and hurt your chances of winning, particularly if you do it repeatedly over a long period of time.

Don't let anybody else carry your rabbits that way, either. When it's time to put your rabbit on the table, at some shows you may carry your own stock, and at others there may be people appointed. Make sure they carry your rabbits properly. Most are briefed on this, but it's surprising how many breeders still handle their prize show specimens as if they were fryers.

Coping with Small Doors

If your rabbits are cooped in cages with small doors, as is, unfortunately, sometimes the case, you may have difficulty getting the rabbit out. There may not be enough clearance to pick up the rabbit correctly. To avoid catching one of its legs on the door, or losing some fur on the wire, do this:

Grasp the rabbit around the back of the head with one hand with your index finger between its ears and extending to the forehead. With the other hand support its hindquarters, extending your thumb into the groin. Then turn the rabbit on its back and you will find you can slide him through the door immobile and without injury or loss of fur. There is no sense in conditioning the rabbit for weeks or months only to lose fur during the show.

If you are responsible for carrying your own rabbits to the judging table, listen for your breed to be announced. At each table a breed chairman, who is a club member, will call for the various classes. If not, you will find a recording secretary or a person working for his judge's license and assisting the judge, who will notify exhibitors of the classes to be brought to the table. When your breed is called, and you have carried your entries and their cards to the table, take a position opposite the judge and watch closely while saying nothing.

Etiquette of the Show Table

Quiet is important for two reasons. The recording secretary and all the exhibitors at the table want to hear the judge's remarks. How he assesses each rabbit is really why they all came today, and they don't want to miss a word of it, even though the essentials are recorded on each card by the recording secretary. The other reason is simply the etiquette of the show table. There should be no remarks about the ownership of this or that rabbit. This judge should have no more identification of each rabbit than its show or coop number. He doesn't want to know and nobody else should know who owns each rabbit.

Let's say we have a class of eight senior bucks. The judge and his assistant check them all for any disqualifications and eliminations, all the while assessing their relative merits. Finding no reason to eliminate or disqualify any, the judge then begins to place them, mentally at first, and perhaps only in two main groups of four each—four off the table first and four to stay.

Soon he's comparing each to the other and to the standard, which he may have open and may be referring to. Number eight goes off first, then seven, six, five, four and so on, but you begin to hold your breath a bit as yours stays on. The comparisons take a little longer now, and the suspense builds. There are only two rabbits left and one is yours. You can tell at a glance that your rabbit is vastly superior. But does the judge have your powers of perception? That other buck is, well, nice and all that, but really, what's taking the judge so long to declare yours the winner? It's getting unbearable. What can he be thinking about? What is taking him so long? It looks like you've got it. But wait, he's looking the other one over again. You know that when he reaches for the right ear of the other rabbit to read its number off for second place that yours will be the winner. But he hasn't done it yet, and the suspense is killing you.

This is what we call fun at the rabbit show. That's really what the show is all about. We spend months waiting for this form of torture. And we revel in it. We love it.

A prize-winning Rex rabbit and proud owner.

He Did It!

Well, breathe easy now, and let the smile slide out. Your buck is first and is held for deciding Best of Variety and possibly Best of Breed. Now senior does, junior bucks, and junior does. Then the other varieties in the breed. He takes out the four "bests." Your buck is still there, having been chosen best in his variety over the senior doe and the junior pair. Will he make it? If not, you want to hope a doe is best, because then your buck and the other bucks will be eligible for best opposite. If another buck is chosen, yours is all done. Close, but no cigar. Oh, it wouldn't be that bad—you already won the class, and with it a grand championship leg. But Best of Breed—that's what we all want to win. It lies before you now—the chance for the trophy, the satisfaction of knowing that all your weeks and months of breeding and conditioning and planning and scheming have paid off. This is the moment you've been waiting for. I sure hope you win.

Author and Chocolate Tan.

About the Author

Bob Bennett breeds Tan rabbits and Florida White rabbits at his home in Shelburne, Vermont, where he also grows a big vegetable garden each year. He is Director of Communications for Vermont's largest electric utility.

He has been a newspaper reporter and editor, a magazine editor, a public relations and advertising executive with oil and pharmaceutical companies, as well as the national sales manager for a publishing company's series of livestock books.

He has been a director of the American Rabbit Breeders Association and was the originator and first editor of its official magazine, **Domestic Rabbits,** which he named.

Bob is a frequent speaker before groups of rabbit raisers and industry organizations, and has served as a consultant to the Boy Scouts of America and to feed and equipment companies in the rabbit field. He is the author of the rabbit management chapter of the **Merck Veterinary Manual.** He raised his first rabbits, New Zealands, in 1948.

Appendix

In this appendix I'm going to give you some hints and tips that have helped me in my rabbit projects of various kinds. I started with rabbits in 1948 and while I haven't had them continuously, I've had them more years than I enjoy contemplating. You'd be amazed at the things you learn over these years.

First, be sure to start out with the best rabbits and equipment you can afford. It's much better to pass up the offer of free sub-standard rabbits and equipment than to take them.

Rabbit Records

Second, keep records. Each rabbit should have a hutch card. These are free at feed stores. Record pertinent data faithfully. Pedigrees should be kept. You don't have to buy certificates. You can make pedigrees out on any kind of paper. Make one out for each rabbit. When you sell a rabbit, make out a pedigree in duplicate. If you keep a copy, you will be in a position to recommend another rabbit to expand the herd.

A stock record book is a good idea. Get a notebook and list each breeder you have. Record its sire and dam, date of birth, sex, ear number. Put down any remarks about it, such as its body type. Keep another notebook and list all your customers with name, address, phone number, and what they bought and when. They will be a prime source for new sales when you need to sell more rabbits. As you progress, you might even mail them all periodic sales letters, followed by phone calls. This can really pay off.

A Rabbit Routine

Work out a system for rabbit keeping. Establish a routine. I feed my rabbits every night between 7 and 9 p.m. I mate them on Saturdays and Sundays. I put in nest boxes on weekends, too, because litters are born on Tuesdays and Wednesdays. With such a routine, you don't forget nest boxes, or to keep things quiet at kindling time.

Remember these key points:

MATING

Take the doe to the buck, not the other way around. Watch for mating to take place. Seeing is believing. Mate does and bucks at 5-6 months of age for such small breeds as Florida Whites; 6-8 months for New Zealand-size rabbits. Be sure to record the date.

TEST-MATING

At a week to 10 days after mating, take doe back to buck. If she growls and resists, she is **probably** pregnant. If she accepts buck, record the date because some does will accept the buck even if they are pregnant.

PALPATION

At 2 weeks after mating, test-mate again. Then palpate. Place doe on a flat surface. Hold skin over shoulders with one hand. Slide other hand under abdomen and feel **gently** for marble-sized objects along **lower sides** of abdomen.

STRAW VOTE

At 28 days after mating, which is time to give the doe a nest box, place a handful of straw on her hutch floor. If she picks it up and carries it around, she is doubtless pregnant. If she does this at about 18 days after mating, however, she may **not** be pregnant, but may have a false or pseudo-pregnancy. In such a case, remate her.

NEST BOX

This goes in on the 28th day after mating. If you aren't sure she's pregnant, give her the box anyway. Better safe than sorry. This is a good time to give the doe small amounts of succulent green feed or roots. Note her consumption of pellets at this time. She may stop eating. This is a good sign she is pregnant. It's also a good sign to give her the greens, which will coax her to eat.

KINDLING

Keep things quiet on the 31st day after mating. Keep kids, dogs, cats, visitors, and other distractions away from the doe. Keep yourself away, too, except to make a judicious inspection the morning after kindling (most kindlings take place at night). If you find any babies out of the nest box, put them in. Make sure all are together. Sometimes a doe will have them on both ends of the box. Put them in one nest, even if you have to fashion it yourself out of the straw and the fur she has pulled.

Problems

I like to divide up the problems you are likely to encounter like this:

1. Health problems, preventive and treatable.
2. Breeding problems (like they won't).
3. People problems (family, neighbors, town officials).

Health

DIARRHEA

Make all feed changes gradual. Watch droppings. At first sign of diarrhea, remove water and any greens. Feed dry hay, dry bread, dry oatmeal (rolled oats). Emtryl is a good preventive. Obtain from farm supply or mail order dealer or see supply information in this book.

COCCIDIOSIS

Once a month, treat drinking water with sulfa quinoxaline. **Not** sulfa methazine. Obtain from farm supply store or mail order house. Follow directions. If no directions are given for rabbits, use directions for poultry. Or use feed pellets medicated with sulfa quinoxaline in accordance with directions. Coccidia are ever-present in all rabbits but this routine should keep them suppressed to a level so low as to be no problem.

EAR MITES

Rabbits raised in all-wire hutches hardly ever get ear mites. If they do, drop a few drops of salad oil (cooking oil) in each ear. This will smother the mites and loosen crusty scales. Check every couple of days and keep adding drops of oil until ears are completely clean.

SORE HOCKS

If rabbits should wear the fur off their foot pads and develop sore feet, treat with Preparation H or similar ointment. Put a board in the hutch for the rabbit to rest on. This should clear up in a few weeks or sooner. When selecting rabbits to buy or keep, choose from among those with well-furred footpads.

COLDS

If rabbits should develop a sneezing problem, treat with Neoterramycin in drinking water. Obtain Neoterramycin where you buy sulfa quinoxaline or see information about supplies in back of this book. If colds persist, use Combiotic, also from same source. Combiotic is also good for cuts, abscesses, and even in conjunction with ointment when treating sore hocks.

OFF FEED

If rabbits refuse to eat, tempt with greens or roots after first making certain of adequate water supply. Rabbits won't eat dry feed if they can't drink.

BUCK TEETH

Malloclusion or buck teeth or wolf teeth are indicated by one pair of front teeth, usually the bottom, overlapping the other. Rabbits' teeth grow continuously. They wear them down by gnawing. If they don't meet, they don't wear down. This can be caused either by heredity or by catching them on cage wire and pulling them out of alignment. Cut them off with wire cutters or dog toenail clippers. If they don't grow back properly, dispose of the animal. Buck teeth are first indicated by the animal becoming wet around the mouth. Keep a sharp eye on your rabbits at feeding time.

Breeding Problems

Don't let does get too fat. Don't let bucks get too hot in summer. If does don't accept bucks, swap hutches. Put him in hers. Leave overnight. Take her back to her own hutch where buck is waiting. Having acquired each other's scent, mating should occur. This also works for those rare instances where buck shows no interest. Mate does back to bucks while young litter is still no more than 8 weeks old. Don't let does rest or they may take a permanent vacation. If too fat, give fewer pellets and more dry hay.

HOT WEATHER

In hot summer months, keep bucks cool to prevent temporary sterility. Give them a daytime hutch or improvised cage in a cool basement during hot days. Put them back in their own hutches at night, when it's cooler. Keep all rabbits out of direct sunlight in hot weather. Shade hutches with wet feed sacks (if burlap) or old carpets or towels. Fill a plastic milk jug with water, freeze it and place in hutch in hot weather. Rabbits will lie against it and cool off.

GETTING ALONG

During hot weather, do not move manure around. You will make things smell worse if you shovel it up and remove it at this time. Instead, sprinkle agricultural limestone, either in granular or powder form, which is available from your farm supply or garden supply store, right under the hutches a couple of times a week. If that doesn't eliminate the smell, there are commercial odor-suppressing products available. One excellent such product is called Odormute. Your farm supply store is a fine source of such products.

Keep a low profile in the neighborhood. Don't make your rabbits obvious. Out of sight, out of mind. My rabbits never smell until my kid punches your kid, so maintain good neighbor relations. If nextdoor or backyard neighbors know about your rabbits (and they need not, necessarily), be sure to provide them with an occasional fryer as a good neighbor gesture. Or, if you have a gardener for a neighbor, give him some manure (composted and dry, if possible—at least in a plastic bag or closed garbage can). Keep children away. Neighbor's kids can be a problem, but the low profile takes care of it, usually. Keeping your rabbits secluded usually keeps them safe. Dogs can be a nuisance. Chase every single dog out of your yard at all times and you probably won't have a dog problem. A fence or shed for your rabbits is the best solution. Make sure your own dog leaves them alone.

THE AUTHORITIES

Find out what the zoning laws are in your town. **Don't** announce to the town clerk that you want to keep rabbits or any other animals. **Do** ask for a copy of **all** the town ordinances. It's either free or costs only a dollar or two. Take it home and read it and decide for yourself whether it lets you raise the number of rabbits you want. Again, keep a low profile and good neighbor relations **regardless** of the zoning laws or other ordinances. You may raise them in violation of the law if you do it wisely. You may not get away with following the letter of the law if you don't. If somebody is out to get you, they will find a way. Don't give them a reason.

Supplies

You should be able to obtain rabbitry supplies and equipment, as well as additional information, from your farm supply or feed store. If your dealer doesn't have what you want, he will probably order it for you. Furthermore, he can give you tips on use of the products he sells. It is in his best interest that you have a well-equipped rabbitry and that your rabbits have everything they need for first rate health and nutrition.

If you don't find your feed store helpful, however, I can supply you with a list of mail-order rabbitry supply houses that can ship you what you need. Usually their catalogs are free or no more than a dollar. Because of company moves, address changes, catalog price changes, and the arrival of new companies (which is occurring rapidly as the industry expands), such lists go out of date faster than books can be reprinted or revised. Then again, there is always the early copy in a library or the back of a shelf in the bookstore.

Therefore, I have found it useful to send out an updated list of such suppliers. I can provide you with names and addresses of equipment suppliers, rabbit suppliers, book suppliers, and the current addresses of the American Rabbit Breeders Association and the Specialty Clubs, such as the American Federation of New Zealand Breeders.

All I ask is you send me a **stamped, self-addressed envelope for reply.** If you have a specific question, I will try to answer it briefly or refer you to a complete answer source. Write me at the address at the end of this section.

Breeding Stock

If you are unable to locate breeding stock of the desired breed, you may also write me for recommendations of U.S. and Canadian breeders. Please enclose a stamped, self-addressed envelope and state the breed or breeds in which you are interested.

Books on Raising Rabbits

I recommend the following books. I have written some and read the others.

Bennett, Bob. **Raising Rabbits the Modern Way.** Pownal, Vermont: Garden Way Publishing, 1975. 158 pages, illustrated. During the past nine years this book has been the best-selling volume on the subject of rabbit raising, with about 130,000 copies in print. While I feel it is now time to read the one you are holding, you may want to go back over this standard work.

Bennett, Bob. **The T.F.H. Book of Pet Rabbits.** Neptune, N.J.: T.F.H. Publishing Co., 1982. 77 pages, 8½ × 11, completely illustrated with full-color photographs and of special interest to serious rabbit raisers and pet owners alike because of the pictures, taken by the world's best photographers of rabbits and beautifully printed. It is also a complete manual for the owner of a single pet rabbit.

Bennett, Bob. **Build Rabbit Housing.** Pownal, Vermont: Garden Way Publishing, 1983. Contains 32 pages of information about building and equipping rabbitries, along with excellent line drawings.

Bennett, Bob. **Rabbit Raising.** Irving, Texas: Boy Scouts of America, 1974. More than 25,000 copies sold and more than 8,000 Boy Scouts have earned the Rabbit Raising Merit Badge with the help of this official manual. It is handy and inexpensive to give to new breeders with the sale of breeding stock.

Cheeke and Patton. **Rabbit Production.** Danville, Ill.: Interstate Publishing, 1982. This is an update of **Domestic Rabbit Production,** originally written by George Templeton and revised by two researchers at Oregon State University, with chapters contributed by Lukefahr and McNitt, also researchers. Textbookish and technical, but has much information worth the effort of reading.

Members of the American Rabbit Breeders Association. **Official Guidebook.** Bloomington, Ill.: ARBA, 1910, with many revisions, including one in 1984.

Members of the American Rabbit Breeders Association. **Domestic Rabbit Cookbook,** Bloomington, Ill.: ARBA, 1980. Contains 285 recipes tested and contributed by ARBA members.

Members of the American Rabbit Breeders Association. **Standard of Perfection,** Bloomington, Ill.: ARBA, 1981. Contains standards of all recognized breeds on 190 pages with 179 illustrations. Indispensable book for the fancier.

Kellogg, Kathy. **Home Tanning & Leathercraft Simplified.** Charlotte, Vermont: Williamson Publishing, 1984. Complete, illustrated home tanning how-to for your rabbit skins, plus excellent fur craft methods and projects. Here's how to add another dimension to rabbit raising. Contains 200 pages with 80 illustrations and photos.

If you are unable to obtain these books from stores where good books are sold, I will send you a list of current prices and addresses. I can also supply information about joining the American Rabbit Breeders Association and the specialty clubs for each breed.

To obtain this information, please send a stamped, self-addressed envelope and clearly state what information you would like to receive. Write Bob Bennett, One Governors Lane, Dept. RRS, Shelburne, Vermont 05482.

Index

C

Carrying cage(s), 77–78, 169
Colony raising, 45
Cooking with rabbits, 15–20
    recipes, 17–20
Crossbreds, 33

D

Diarrhea, 41, 100, 156, 169, 180
Diet, 32. See also **Feed**(ing)
Direct sunlight, affect on fur, 155
Domestic Rabbits magazine, 119, 158–9
Door(s), hutches, 66–68
    hangers, 60
    latches, 60, 67
Dwarfs, 117

F

Feed(ing), 79–86
    amounts to supply, 94–95
    costs, 86–87
    establishing a routine, 95
    for prime fur and flesh condition, 155–7
Feeders, 69–70
    hopper feeder, 81, 94
    hay rack, 70, 95
Feed/meat conversion ratio, 32
Fertility problems, 96, 101, 152, 181
Flemish Giant, 23, 27, 137
Florida White(s), 9, 28, 30, 33, 36, 60, 86, 94, 95, 100, 110, 137
    characteristics, 25–27, 43
Fur. **See also** Pelts
    brushes, 158
    -chewing, 155
    coloring/marking, 139–40
    criteria for judging, 124, 145
    direct sunlight on, 155
    prime condition of, 166

G

Grand champions, 132, 154
    management for, 152–8
    selection for, 164–7
Gestation. **See** Pregnancy
Guide Book of the American Dutch Rabbit Club, 145

H

Hay racks, 70, 95
Health problems, 180–1
Housing, 45–69. **See also** Hutch(es)
Hutch(es), 45. **See also** Housing
    advantages, all-wire, 49
    arrangements, 55–57
    building plan, medium breeds, 62–69
    building plan, smaller breeds, 69
    calculating floor space, 60–62
    for champions, 155
    converted mink cages, 50
    how to build, 59–69
    hung from roof, joists, 49, 55, 57
    for larger rabbitry, 68
    selling, 88–89, 108, 119–22
    wire mesh box, 47
Hutch card(s), 31, 97, 99, 147–8, 178
Hutch record(s). **See** Hutch card(s)
Hybrids. **See** crossbreds
Hybrid vigor, 27

I

Inbreeding. **See** linebreeding

J

Judging
    body types, 124, 144–5
    fur, 124–5
    your own stock, 162–5

K

Kindling, 99–100, 178

L

Leg certificates, 131. **See also** Grand Champions
Licenses (to sell rabbit meat), 110
Linebreeding, 150–1
Litter(s), 99–100
    weaning, 101–2
Lockley, R. M., 101
Lops, 117, 137

M

N

P